Heart on the Page

on the

Page

A Portable Writing Workshop

Wendy Brown-Baez

HEART ON THE PAGE: A PORTABLE WRITING WORKSHOP is an inspirational guide for both individual writers and writing instructors who teach in institutions, non-profit organizations, and healing centers. It interweaves stories of workshops held in community spaces with practical advice on how to guide, encourage and inspire writers who may not think of themselves as writers but have a story to tell. Specific poems and prompts to access intuitive guidance and unblock creativity are interwoven with writing exercises. Wendy offers tips and suggestions on how to engage participants with physical or emotional health challenges and shares stories about how the power of words creates transformation and change.

Writing and sharing stories activates the ability to find meaning after trauma, loss, or transition. This book is a resource for staff or volunteers to incorporate therapeutic writing as a tool for healing, self-awareness and creative expression for their clients and/or for self-care while providing care for others. The book concludes with additional advice about taking the next step from spontaneous freewriting to the craft of memoir.

Heart on the Page is a compilation of the life's work of Wendy Brown-Báez, creator of Writing Circles for Healing. She has facilitated writing workshops for more than fifteen years in community spaces including human service and arts non-profits; institutions such as schools, prisons and libraries; and healing centers, spiritual centers and yoga studios. These poems and prompts were used successfully in her workshops. Wendy has facilitated workshops in the following organizations as well as others:

All About the Journey

Abbot Northwestern Hospital Heart Group

Amazon Bookstore Collective

Banfille-Locke Center for the Arts

Black Dog Café

Boneshaker Books

Celebrate Yourself Women's Retreat

Common Grounds Café

Cornerstone

Eastside Freedom Library

Eat My Words Bookstore

El Colegio High School

Face to Face Charter High School

Harriet Tubman

Healing Elements

Hennepin County Central Library

Hennepin County Walker Library

Jacobs' Well Women's Retreat

Lennox Community Center

MCTC

Minneapolis Community Ed

Mn Prison Writing Workshop

NE Wellness

Opposable Thumbs Bookstore

Pathways: A Healing Center

Quartrefoil Library

Resource Center for the Americas

SafeZone

Saint Paul Almanac

Santa Fe Community Yoga

Springhouse Spiritual Center

Subtext Books

The Aliveness Project

The Golden Deli and Café

UMN Hospital

Unity Minneapolis

Wellstone Center

Women's Spirituality and Health Conference

Acknowledgements:

Why We Write: The Wounded and Enduring, Poets & Writers Magazine 2014

The Aliveness Project, The Compassion Anthology, online, 2016

Take Care of Yourself: how to deal with emotional overload A Walk Around the Writer's Block The Loft blog

- Excerpt from *Waking: A Memoir of Trauma and Transformation* by Matthew Sanford, Rodale Books by permission of the author © 2008 Matthew Sanford
- Poem Joan Logghe "Famous Kisses" © Joan Logghe by permission of the author
- Poem: Dobby Gibson, "Upon Discovering My Entire Solution to the Attainment of Immortality Erased from the Blackboard Except the Word 'Save'" from *Polar*. Copyright © 2005 by Dobby Gibson. Reprinted with the permission of The Permissions Company, LLC on behalf of Alice James Books, www.alicejamesbooks.org.
- Excerpt from *Writing with At-Risk Youth: The Pongo Teen Writing Method* by Richard Gold, Rowman & Littlefield, by permission of author © 2014 Richard Gold

Contents

FOREWORD

To fully understand Wendy Brown Baez as a teacher, you must begin with a bus. Start with a bus that travels to prisons, hospitals, high schools, churches, and libraries, for Wendy goes to all of those places and she does so via the crowded seats of a city bus. She fills her tote bag with books and writings (others and her own), an e-reader, copies of *The Sun*, *Poet's & Writers*, and a bag of peanut M&M's. She hauls her supplies from the suburbs to the city center, to the far margins of the metro—sometimes all in one day.

Do you realize how far outside of town most prisons are situated? Do you know how hard it must be to face a room full of people who've just lost a loved one to suicide? Nothing about Wendy's work is simple. Add to the mix the fact that she teaches for little or no compensation and it's easy to understand how, if you weren't wise-hearted and determined, it might be easier to just stay home.

Yet Wendy gets on the bus. She's knocked on my door countless times en route to one prison or another through our shared work with the Minnesota Prison Writing Workshop. To arrive on time, Wendy sometimes leaves her house at six AM and travels for over an hour before walking blocks to the next bus, or train, or coworker that will ferry her to the final leg of her trip. Despite such complications, she's the first to volunteer for a class. She is never late. She never complains. To be sure, if you offer her a ride home, she will say *yes* before the offer is fully out of your mouth. Wendy does not love the bus. I don't think she enjoys hauling ingredients for a group's potluck (nachos) or waiting under awnings on winter days (20 below), or the profanity that flies out of kids' mouths (@#*!). (The later she always mentions to me after I've let a few words slip myself.) She's the tenderest-made-of-steel woman I've met; nothing stops her from getting to her classes. Not even security protocol in a maximum-security prison.

When Wendy teaches with MPWW, her journey doesn't end when she arrives at the facility. Her next obstacle is to clear security. The corrections officer checks her bag. Checks her ID. Send her through the metal detector. Wands her hip. Stamps her hand. Signs her in. Opens the gates. Her journey may have begun three hours prior, but she is only just now getting close to seeing her students.

When Wendy does finally walk through the door of her classroom, her students often act as though they are the ones who have traveled far to reach this moment. They experience their time in Wendy's writing classes as *their* journey—as of course they should, as of course it is. She makes sure it's so. She checks her stress at the door and holds space for people in tangible ways. She forms a circle, lets participants know what to expect, and begins by handing out a poem. The poem is carefully chosen, literature that Wendy offers as both prompt and gift.

Look, will you, at the curated list of poets in this book: Kim Addonizio, Edward Hirsch, Dorianne Laux, Naomi Shahib Nye, Mark Doty, among many others. This is a teacher who demands gravity and art from her teaching tools, who hand-selects poems that will sing for the people in the room, whether these people are children or the dying or incarcerated. She selects poems, I should say, that acknowledge wounds and affirm our humanity.

Then she lets the poems do their work. Her classes quite deliberately offer poetry as a portal to what Camus calls "a trek through the detours of art to recapture those one or two moments when [our] heart first opened." Her classroom is quiet, and the pathway is laid in words by word by stanza. It's then that Wendy invites students to write, and hear, and be heard. Or to be silent. In that invitation, participants begin to discover the work they're there to do.

Many of Wendy's students have experienced abuse, addiction, death, suicide, cancer and on and on. For many, this may be the first time their stories have made it fully to their consciousness, let alone the page. They may uncover and write of their resentment about caring for a terminally ill loved one. Being thrown out on the street. Of losing a daughter to suicide. Of their own violent crimes and remorse. Wendy has undoubtedly heard stories about how the victim became the perpetrator or how fathers who were left have left their sons. It isn't easy work.

All the while, Wendy sits up straight with quiet strength—full of patience, absent of judgement. It's a hallmark of her teaching. Her students notice this. While it may sound like a simple thing, I'd argue it's what allows them to first engage and later persist as writers. One of her students, Dara, once wrote in an evaluation that Wendy's classroom felt safe because, she "took control of the room with a strong, yet gentle voice, which commanded respect and showed authority." That's nice in any class, but it's especially important in a prison. Another student, Wally, an experienced writer in our program, said he took Wendy's class hoping just to be given space to write. He didn't expect craft lessons to sneak up from the surface of their discussions each time the group met, but they did, and it's had a powerful impact on his writing. Another student, Tony, a man who has taken many, many classes with Wendy, once stood before a room of a hundred onlookers at his class reading and said: "Wendy is amazing. This woman can handle *anything.*" And it's touching in part because he was three times her size but drawing on her strength. Mostly it was moving because it was so clearly true.

When I first started traipsing through Minnesota's prisons with Wendy, I assumed her sturdy calm came from working with such a wide range of students. She's the only writer I've known who has experience working with the dying and bereaved, at-risk kids, shattered parents, battered women, and men convicted of abuse. She's taught people from ages fourteen to ninety. This month alone, Wendy will teach a class of adult women at Shakopee Prison, a mixed community of students and family members in the wake of a suicide at an at-risk high school, and religion education to a multi-age class. While I'm sure that range and experience explains some of her magic, Wendy's true gift comes from something deeper than practice and more earth-worn than pedagogy. Hers is the sort of calm that can't be taught or borrowed or undone, this deeply centered, unshakeable confidence that comes from life experience.

It was in reading *Heart on the Page* that I finally and fully understood Wendy's teaching. Her approach to writing—while full of craft tools and inventive prompts—is not born in the academy. Thank goodness for that because we need all types. It's rooted in life, and loss and, importantly, the will to find a path back to light. Before she was teaching all over the state of Minnesota, Wendy was on the streets, in homelessness, as part of a commune lost in the deserts of Israel. She suffered the death of a partner and a son. Enduring even one of these things might have decimated most of us. Wendy's spirit isn't the sort to curl up in fetal position and turn out the lights.

"Life wanted life," Robert Hass says.

"We have to survive," Cheryl Strayed reminds us. "We have to."

And so she has. *Life wanted life.* For Wendy, rebuilding happened through words. She wrote her way back, not just to surviving, but to vibrancy. She developed a writing practice, which is to say, she developed a practice of turning pain into art. Out of that process we see Wendy's heart-battered strength. Can there be any greater generosity than to make from your tragedies something that benefits others? Her peace, as I see it, comes not just from surviving, but from weaving a luminous life after loss. She proceeds with an almost unshakeable certainty that, come what may, words will always repair.

This is what fills her classroom. It's what her students speak of when they fill out evaluations and thank her behind the podium of their class readings. Her students have inherited Wendy's very faith. They accept her resilience and her craft guidance and her quiet resolve and they set their own pens to work. Almost without exception, they write. Even when their resources are worn thin, they write into the raw spots as writers must. Which is all to say, they borrow Wendy's stubborn grace until they find their own. And then they're off.

And so is Wendy, to her next class: at an elementary school, a homeless shelter, a hospital. She'll load her tote bag and throw it over her arm, pay the bus fare, gather participants into a circle, share a poem, and offer her attention. What she teaches people, as well as what they've taught her, is inside these pages. Reading this book won't just make you a better teacher or a better writer—though it will do that. It will make you a more capacious human.

Read Wendy's story. Heed her advice. She's put in a lot of miles to learn and live so deeply and well. In fact, she's traveled more than anyone I know.

Jennifer Bowen Hicks

Founder, Artistic Director, Minnesota Prison Writing Workshop

Preface

F or ten years, the best years of my youth, the years when I had energy and desire, I lived in a commune. These were my childbearing years, the years when I was skinny and strong, with plenty of idealism and chutzpah. I learned the rigors of self-discipline, to take last place and to be of service to the poor. I learned to live on one strong cup of coffee and one meal, to baste a turkey all night in the kitchen with an ex-con and not be conned by his charm, to travel with just my thumb, a Bible tucked in my bag, and faith that all humankind was created to "love one another". I learned to be grateful for daily miracles such as a hot pot of tea while on the road or a heart-to-heart conversation around the campfire. I learned that a life of compassion, idealism, and service did not mean that life was always merciful.

While my best friend and I were in New York City gathering money for airfare to join our brothers and sisters in Europe, we made friends with a young man named Fred. One day he told us that the reason he liked us was that we transcended the darkness on a daily basis. We wore embroidered Mexican blouses and wrapped up against the cold in *rebozo*s. Mine was woven of purple, pink and turquoise and hers was sunset-orange and earth-brown, in contrast to New Yorkers who wore black, navy, and occasionally gray. I think about his perception of us. Based on our colorful appearance and our lively conversations, he believed that we were warding off the demons of doubt, fear, despair, greed, selfishness, and vanity. Little did I know that the struggle to transcend the darkness within would go on, year after year. Rare moments of joy, momentarily comprehending mystical teachings, and the sense of connection with divinity, would have to compensate for the ordinary moments of meals to be cooked, laundry to be schlepped to the laundromat, unpaid bills, heartbreak, doctor visits, and the grinding of daily poverty. My life was later filled with love so strong it was terrifying; of grief so deep, it felt like an abyss; of hopes crushed and the ordinary task of putting one foot in front of the other to get up, go to work, pay the bills, make the meals, and soothe my wounded spirit almost more than I could do.

I know many of us faced depression those first fragile years after the group unraveled and we had to de-program ourselves from "group think" to be ourselves. For me, falling in love swept me out of the painfulness of betrayal, the devastating realization I had given my life and the lives of my children into the hands of a crazy person. First I fell in love with stretching into freedom, then it was individual lovers who came into my life, and after I returned to the states, it was the love of writing that kept despair at bay. I signed up for an extended university writing class in my hometown. I had written poems, short stories and novels for years before I joined the commune. I had stopped completely, feeling my work was not masterful enough to hold up to the scrutiny of "perfection" that we were coached to attain. The stories of my experiences were overflowing and I felt compelled to get as much of it down on paper as I could. It was therapeutic and healing and gave me fresh perspectives on the person I had been and the one I was on my way to becoming.

Eventually, I left my hometown to move back to the Southwest and there, I reconnected with the love of my life, Michael Woehler. He was gregarious, funny, warm-hearted, affectionate, honest, and lived his life in a creative fury. We fell deeply in love, soulmates and explorers. After a few months as we headed into winter, his mood changed to deep depression. I demanded that he see a doctor and for the first time despite years of mood swings, he was diagnosed with bi-polar disorder. The next eight years were a roller-coaster of manic highs when he stayed up all night, blasted CDs at full volume, disappeared out of state, spent recklessly, and became aggressive and angry if I tried to calm him down, and lows that sucked the air out of the room while he spent all day in bed or watched TV, unable to open his mail or choose a change of clothes. I lived in a constant state of fear after he told me he wanted to die. It is hard to describe my anguish, not knowing what part of the roller coaster ride was coming next.

It was during this time that I joined two writing groups. One was a women's poetry group and the other was Write Action, a group led by Joan Logghe for anyone with health challenges. These would cushion my grief when he finally took his life.

Michael's death released me from the depression that had slipped onto my own shoulders. A wave of creative inspiration uplifted me. I self-produced a poetry CD, had a launch party, traveled to the East Coast and the West Coast to promote it, and honed my poetry performance style. I rejoiced in the birth of grandchildren and redecorated the apartment we had shared to suit my own style. I celebrated friendships with dinner parties and generated poetry events with my women's poetry group.

When tragedy struck, it came as a complete shock. Three years after Michael's death, my younger son died also by suicide, and my life shattered. It would take many years to pick up those pieces. I was filled with deep anger—anger at myself, anger at him, anger at God. I was left with a huge burden of guilt—that I hadn't seen it coming, that I hadn't tried to stop it. On top of this, I had married a gay Mexican man in order to help secure his medical care in the states and had moved out of the condo to live with him. Defeated by paperwork, he returned to Mexico. I was homeless in more ways than just a space to live in. I felt not only bereft but adrift. Life no longer made sense to me. I could only put one foot in front of the other, day by day. I could not pray and I couldn't write. Or perhaps I denied myself the solace writing could have given me out of sheer hopelessness.

I moved to Minnesota when my son requested help with child-care. Despite my profound grief, I continued to look for ways to activate my life-force—poetry had once been my passion and my calling. I attended a workshop and had a revelation: I could make my story into a work of art. I could transform it and give it meaning through the act of writing. The idea of writing circles came to me soon after that. How could I integrate my passion for words with the desire to be of service? I had experienced traumatic grief, I had facilitated writing workshops for years, and I had been trained to listen as a hospice volunteer. I started writing poetry again after months of resistance. How could I honor Sam? How could I make meaning out of his death? Here was a dream to propel me out of the depths of grief into something I could offer, something true to my own soul. I could facilitate writing groups for people who have suffered or are suffering. I could help people to access their deepest thoughts, fears, and hopes. *I have been through it all.* I was still on the quest for answers and I found them everywhere, even in the heart of a stranger as we leaned closer in empathy. Everyone has a story, I soon discovered. Everyone has grief somewhere in their family story and finds courage to go on, keeping their raft afloat on the sea of life.

HOW THIS BOOK IS ORGANIZED:

I begin with my own story: why writing is a tool for my own healing. I share tips and advice on how to create intimacy and safety for writing with those who may be experiencing a range of emotions and may be in a time of life-altering change. My personal experience is that people are drawn to writing workshops when they have something urgent to tell but may not yet know what it is. I have heard participants say, "I have never written this story before" or "I have never told this to anyone before." I tell stories of my own search for healing, meaning, connection and transformation and stories of how I came to work within particular organizations and why. I share experiences in writing with groups focused on specific topics, such as self-care for care-givers; healing during illness; writing through abuse, grief, homelessness, or remorse; writing with teens and incarcerated writers; and writing for spiritual exploration. Each section lists specific poems and prompts that were useful to me as suggestions to jumpstart your own writing or to lead writing in a group. All of these poems are available on-line. By no means are these lists exhaustive. Every day I find new poems and new prompts but these have opened hearts and minds every time I used them. I include some of my own responses to prompts.

I explain how to take care of yourself when unsettling emotions surface, either from what you hear or what you are writing, and the value of poetry as a key to enter intuitive writing.

The second section is about writing memoir, the nuts and bolts of the difficult task of revealing yourself when you speak your truth.

The book ends with a list of books to encourage, deepen, and inspire your writing from writers of every genre. Writing can be a lonely path although there are many of us along for the journey. Writing together in a group is one way to keep the juices flowing or grease the wheels but ultimately to sustain a writing life, you must also write on your own whether or not you think you have the time or space, the privacy or the right equipment. I have seen stacks of paper filled from one edge of the paper to the other with miniscule handwriting from incarcerated writers who write on their bunks in the dead of night because it is the only time they can find quiet. I know it is possible to honor yourself as a writer no matter if you are published or if you have ever earned a dime. Writing is a way to not only hear your own thoughts and discover who you are, it is a way to send a message to the world, even if it is tucked into a bottle and thrown into a vast sea. I believe that writing is a practice just like any art form and the more you practice, the better you become and the more you practice, the more you want to practice. For many in a workshop, it may be a once in a lifetime experience but can set change in motion. For others, it will lead to a lifetime of wielding the pen for self-discovery, revelation, imagination, and joy. For all of you who have picked up this book, I believe the light shines in each one of us and we each have a purpose in this world. For me, writing has always been both a way to explore the unknown and to keep that light burning. I rejoice in the power of words to articulate what is deepest within. My motto is, "The shortest bridge between us is a story" and I hope this book inspires you to tell yours.

PART 1:
WRITING WORKSHOPS

How to Begin

I begin with a circle. Circles have power. In a circle a resonance takes place between us as we share support and encouragement. In a circle we are equals. When we hear what others have written, we hear our own thoughts: our fears, worries, painful truths, regrets and failures, moments of gladness and times of resiliency. When we read aloud, we hear our own words, as if for the first time. If we have just written them, they may seem raw and emotionally vulnerable. How many times have I heard a participant in a writing group say: "This isn't very good." Or, "I didn't follow directions, I didn't understand the prompt, this is just rambling," and then proceed to read something astonishingly honest, heartfelt, deep, often well written. The emotional turmoil coming to the surface may make it hard to recognize the writing's beauty and courage. The vulnerable honesty of the writing connects those of us listening to it. Emotions surface in a way that is organic and so it doesn't feel like the effort we imagine writing must take. Often we do not recognize the power of our own voice, the impact our words have on the rest of the circle. It is a process that is spontaneous, natural and always extraordinary. What arises may be completely unexpected or we may be troubled by something we have needed to articulate.

My experience as a facilitator of writing circles is that we each have a unique voice but common threads run through our writing: being silenced by shame or blame, wounded hearts, loneliness and longing, memories of loss, betrayal and despair, broken promises and lost dreams, choosing to move forward, remembrances of happy times, the talents and gifts we have or want to reclaim, gratitude, and the desire for connection to nature and to each other. Often I feel that someone writes what I wish I had written. I recognize myself. I recognize my strengths and I feel affirmed and validated.

My instructions are to allow spontaneous writing to connect the hand holding the pen to the intuitive right side of the brain and allow what needs to surface to come up. Usually the writing exercise begins with a poem as a way to tap into the right brain. I instruct the participants that they don't have to understand the poem in order to enter the rhythm of language. We don't discuss the poem; we read it around the circle, taking turns, unless it is short or crafted as just one sentence, in which case I might ask someone to read it. Reading aloud is another form of listening and absorbing language, rhythm, and imagery to trigger the imagination. I have noticed that reading aloud is a pleasurable but lost art.

We don't discuss the poem, as this will take us back to the left-brain's analytical linear process. We want to stay with the creative imagination. I suggest a prompt and always give the writers permission to rebel and start with *What I really want to say is...*or *What I notice is...*Maybe another line from the poem might grab their attention. Often poems are chosen deliberately for particular images, words and concepts that I hope will deepen the intuitive process on a subconscious level. I tell the writers that the story we need to tell, the one we are compelled to tell, will come to the surface, especially if we practice spontaneous freewriting on a regular basis.

I write with the group and share my writing. I write in a way that is personal, intimate, honest, and revealing. I call it self-reflective writing. Self-reflective writing owes much to Natalie Goldberg, author of *Writing Down the Bones, Freeing the Writer Within,* and the instructions are simple: keep the pen moving and ignore the critic's voice in your head demanding perfection, cleverness or style while pouring your heart out. Allow the writing to flow naturally. I have learned that although I can write quickly in spontaneous freewriting, I can control the direction my work takes. I start with the same prompts I suggest to the group: What I left behind, what I regret and what I don't, what I didn't know I loved, what brings me joy, etc and reach a place where I can choose to go down one path or another. I can travel deeper into the story of what happened to me or I can change direction to a shift in perspective. I can choose at which angle to view my story: is the glass half empty or half full, can the hurt heart learn forgiveness, can the wound compost into wisdom? I choose the path of an uplifting interpretation deliberately as leader of the group.

I begin by creating a sense of safety and intimacy. The safety is partly due to the fact that we do not critique or workshop in the beginning. If the class is geared toward creating a final piece to be read, we will critique and revise later. The fact that we will not be critiqued gives us safety. Usually I say that positive feedback is okay, such as a line that we appreciate or resonate with or an image that particularly strikes us or is expressed well. At other times, I ask that our only response be, "Thank you." This technique of not commenting feels strange at first, especially to more experienced writers who anticipate and welcome comments and especially new writers who want to be complimented on their writing. It frees us up as writers tremendously. We do not have to respond either emotionally or verbally, either defensively or with gratitude. We are free to simply share and be heard. As we go around the circle, more people share than perhaps would if they thought someone might comment. If the material we are working with is particularly difficult, the instruction to only say "thank you" is helpful for each individual writer and for the group. We don't have to think of what to say, just listen. The next writing exercise will go deeper with more honesty as we experience this freedom to be ourselves.

I create intimacy in the beginning by sharing something personal about myself. If intimacy is one of the most important foundations of the group, that is, if it is writing for healing and not a craft workshop, I share my healing story. I tell them about the death of my partner and how it released a burst of creative energy, followed by the death of my son, which shut down my creativity. Then I say, "Writing is like riding a bicycle. If you have been practicing, whether it is journaling or writing exercises or working on a story or novel, it comes back. I decided to join my writing groups again. This was my routine, they were my friends. I didn't think I could write but I could listen and be part of the group. However, once I had a pen in my hand, it was natural to put it to paper. The writing was emotionally raw and rambling but at least I was writing while in the group. At home, by myself, still nothing was getting onto the page. It would take months before I could access my voice again. Over time, it came back to me, naturally, with deeper meanings and stronger images." By sharing my story, it enables participants to trust me and to have confidence that I will be able to hear their deepest secrets, darkest hours, and most shameful failures. They trust that I won't judge and that I won't be shocked or dismayed by what they share.

I hold the energy and space for the group. I don't consider myself a leader so much as a facilitator although I am also responsible for the well-being of the group and the feeling of relief at the end.

Occasionally even in a short two hour workshop we will witness someone making a break-through. Tears, laughter, and deep sharing will bond the group together and enable the writers to become aware of what may have been holding them back and what they can do to nourish their creative spirits. I thank the participants for their vulnerability and their courage. I remind them that it takes a lot of courage to write and to share their writing. If the session was particularly emotional, I might end with a brief meditation and we might place our hands over our hearts, pat ourselves on the back, visualize a successful project completed, or stand up and shake the energy out.

I bring handouts of poems, writing advice, and inspirations: I call myself "the hand-out queen." I choose a selection of poems to use as jump-starts but I may change course when I hear something from the check in or when we read aloud.

Depending on the group and its purpose, I also bring handouts about the craft of writing, about paying attention, finding voice, how to develop character, tips to inspire and freshen up your writing, dialogue practice, thoughts on memoir, questions to ask yourself to further your writing, how to's and advice from other writers. For workshops that are geared toward writing craft, such as Aspiring Writers, Writing Naturally, Dynamic First Pages, Choices and Conflicts, Telling Your Story, and In Our Own Voices, I bring a page with a list of local writing events and opportunities: where to find readings, retreats and conferences; where to submit; and how to connect with other writers. I try to create catchy titles for my workshops but they don't seem to matter. If someone is looking for a writing class, they will find me.

If you want to teach writing workshops in community organizations, my advice is to call or show up in person. Staff personnel are often overwhelmed with emails and daily administrative tasks. It is likely that they will introduce you to the volunteer coordinator. Having the Minnesota State Arts Board grant smoothed the way for me, as it meant they had only to advertise the workshop to their clients and provide a space since my fee was paid by the grant. Some organizations provided snacks and notebooks. With the grant, I was also able to offer workshops as a tool to help clients for staff and volunteers. I believe that writing can be a tool used by therapists, social workers, counselors and case managers in simple ways, such as a five to ten minute writing to begin a session but I understand the limitations of time. I believe it is worth the effort for organizations to find grant funding to host writing workshops and I also understand that finding enough funding is a constant factor in the ability to provide services for clients. My dream is that funding for workshops could come from the community as we realize the value of healing our inner selves as well as our bodies. It is becoming more acceptable for hospitals and healing centers to consider writing as complementary or integrative medicine.

My hope is that members of the staff of an organization can use this book as a template for their own process of writing as well as with clients, in order to foster creative self-awareness, self-expression, and rejuvenation. Journaling is one resource for accessing one's thoughts and feelings. Using prompts suggested in this book for freewriting may deepen the way you mine the gold of your own unique human expression. I believe it is essential for those in the human service field to practice self-care. Journaling and/or self-reflective writing are excellent avenues to develop self-awareness and to discharge secondary trauma, to recalibrate, refresh and refuel.

Writing for Healing

My healing story begins not with my own healing but with seeking solutions for my companion's depression. Michael's periods of depression seemed endless as he responded negatively to every circumstance. No matter what he was experiencing—excellent food, friends, dancing, traveling—he said he felt terrible. Sometimes he was unable to get out of bed for days at a time. Other times, he was energetic, gregarious, spending money wildly, disappearing for days to other states or even across the border, followed by aggression and anger. With a diagnosis of bi-polar disorder, the puzzle pieces fell into place, but he hated the way medication made him feel. We lived in Santa Fe, New Mexico, a Mecca for alternative healing, and I began to search for alternatives to prescription drugs. *Earthwalks for Health* was part of that search. *Earthwalks for Health* connected us to Indigenous artists and local sages to learn about their traditional spirituality and healing practices. This is how I met Joan Logghe, beloved Santa Fe poet. Joan was the founder of Write Action, a writing support group for people who were HIV positive. As time went on, they either died or became so well, they no longer had the time or inclination to attend, so she opened it up to anyone with a health challenge.

I was writing poetry with another group at the time. I knew how cathartic it was to write my thoughts down and encouraged Michael to attend Joan's group. He found it satisfying to pour out his brutal honesty on paper and not be judged. One week, he couldn't attend because he was going out of town so I suggested that I go and "keep his seat warm." I loved it and we continued attending together weekly. We both felt we had a home where we were supported and accepted. It was energizing to hear common themes go around the circle and to be reassured that coping with Michael's moods was not isolating us.

Joan had worked with Natalie Goldberg and used the same basic writing instruction that so many writing instructors and writing groups would come to rely on: spontaneous timed writing. Pick a time, put pen to the paper and keep it moving, not stopping to consider grammar or sentence structure or even if it makes sense. Natalie Goldberg also writes in *Writing Down the Bones, Freeing the Writer Within,* "go for the jugular. If something comes up in your writing that is scary or naked, dive right into it. It probably has lots of energy."

Joan used poems as prompts. In this way, we entered the rhythm of language. The poetic associations and images we read inspired our own words. I especially appreciated the exposure to poets unfamiliar to me. Joan was compassionate and humorous, non-critical and non-judgmental, and was willing to share her own beautiful honest and vulnerable writing, even if to her it felt "uncooked." From her, I learned that by sharing my own work, I create a sense of intimacy and inspire confidence in others to share. I consider her a friend and a mentor, someone who showed by her example how to lead writing for healing and how to create a safe, welcoming space.

Eventually Michael became more and more mentally unstable and one night he gathered up the courage to end his mental torment by killing himself. I wept until my eyes were swollen shut, but I was released from caregiving and uplifted by a burst of creative energy. To be able to pour out my grieving heart onto the page in the writing groups was cathartic. To know that others were willing to be on the journey, accompanying me through the muck, was lifesaving. From that point on, writing became not only a way of self-expression but a life raft that saved me from drowning. When emotions feel overwhelming, writing helps me to stay focused. Writing helps me to analyze and understand what I am feeling and to make a shift from emotion to clarity.

Ten years later, I received the Minnesota State Arts Board Artist Initiative grant. Pathways was one of my targeted organizations. I led workshops specifically for caregivers to have a break, for self-care. Every other Thursday afternoon became my niche from that time on.

Pathways: A Healing Center offers free mind-body-spirit workshops for clients and their families. The class I offered at Pathways was called Care for the Caregiver. I know the toll that caregiving can take and hoped to offer creative respite. I informed the participants that we are neither a support group nor a writing group with the purpose of improving writing skills but a way to connect to our deep intuition and inner wisdom. I believe that the soul knows what it needs to take care of itself if we listen to our inner voice.

Participants came and went in this writing group, depending on a conflict when other services are offered, energy levels, or the ability to have someone take over their duties. Often the participants had their own health challenges. They may write while propped on pillows on the floor. The caregiving may have happened in the past rather than currently. Word of mouth spread about the benefits of the group and in 2016, I changed the name to Writing for Healing. Since then, at each session we have a group of 6-10 people. Through Pathways, I also had the opportunity to write with patients at the UMN Hospital oncology unit as part of their integrative medicine program. This meant that I was writing with patients who wheeled in a stand holding multiple IVs, family members who are caregivers, staff nurses, and occasionally visitors. More about writing for healing follows this section on writing for caregivers.

The poetry I bring needs to be very accessible. Most of the participants do not read poetry and attention may waver due to physical discomfort. Images from nature are especially appreciated. We take turns reading the stanzas aloud and then I suggest a prompt. We do not critique or workshop our writings. This gives us the freedom to be honest on the page. I'll share an insight or wisdom such as a meditation I use, acknowledgment that care-giving changes our identity, or the opportunities that come to us to further our spiritual practice when we feel others, perhaps those we feel closest to or the person we are caring for, do not understand, approve or feel threatened when we take time out from caregiving to be ourselves. I share my own spiritual practice of paying attention to my thoughts and attitudes and deliberately changing negativity to positivity. I may suggest writing affirmations. I might comment on how our culture insistently gives us the message that we are not enough when we are not only enough, but miracles. I might share appreciation for writing that is especially moving or has deep wisdom. I might suggest how to develop writing that seems to be the start of something. Others may similarly comment on what has moved them or resonated with them. I always try to uplift the group if the writing has been particularly painful.

Writing opens our hearts so that we can be authentic. Many caregivers and those with health challenges are angry, frustrated, frightened, grieving, and exhausted. Caregivers succumb to being completely available, both emotionally and physically, to the demands of caregiving, and feel they must keep up a strong, cheerful, optimistic façade. People may themselves be coping with an invisible disability and lack of understanding and awareness from others. Even those with obvious health challenges, using a walker for example, may find that others do not understand the depth of their grief over losing their abilities or the intense frustration of losing ways they were self-sufficient. I had one participant whose husband had given away all of their money as his dementia took over and another whose dying husband was in denial and wouldn't let her prepare for a future without him. Participants with environmental sensitivities might complain that ordinary daily activities were a minefield of allergic reactions and the well-meaning but clueless advice of others abrasive.

In our writing group, we can let down the façade and explore what we yearn for, what our passions are, and what gives us solace and spiritual nourishment. We can plan for the future and coach ourselves through fear and grief by being present and reminding ourselves to focus on the present. We remind ourselves of the many gifts we have and the support system of family, friends, and organizations such as Pathways. We write about making choices based on knowing ourselves and accepting our limitations and honoring our vision of what can be. We realize we walk a path of compassion with strength, courage, and wisdom. We learn that others have also walked this path and we have a sense of commonality and community. Our inner resilience becomes more certain and we acknowledge blessings along the way.

TYPICAL WRITING PROMPTS FOR CAREGIVERS

I don't have to be perfect, I just have to—

list all the things you do for yourself, from the smallest thing such as a bubble bath to taking yoga, walking, or calling a friend: how do you raise your vibration?

What brings you joy?

What gives you bliss?

What do you yearn for?

How do you have fun?

What do you do for pleasure?

I promise myself—

What my tears tell me

POEM: Kindness by Naomi Shihab Nye

PROMPT: what I left behind and what I was able to keep—

POEM: Antilamentation by Dorianne Laux

PROMPTS: what I regret and what I don't regret

what you gave me—

POEM: Permission Granted by David Allen Sullivan

PROMPT: I give myself permission to—

POEMS: Rest by Richard Jones, Let Evening Come by Jane Hirshfield

PROMPT: Where do you find solace?

POEM: The Book of Myths by Joy Harjo

PROMPT: my beloved body—

POEM: I'm Going to Start Living like a Mystic by Edward Hirsch

PROMPT: I'm going to start living—

POEM: The Tao of Touch by Marge Piercy

PROMPT: what nourishes me

POEM: Prayer in The Strip Mall, Bangor, Maine by Stuart Kestenbaum

PROMPT: random Love—

POEM: Discovering Gold by Wendy Brown-Baez

PROMPT: bless the coming darkness or discovering gold

POEM: For What Binds Us by Jane Hirshfield

PROMPT: what binds us, scars

POEM: from a Native Elder Teaching Story translated by David Wagoner

PROMPT: Have you ever felt lost / how do you find yourself

POEM: The Singing by Kim Addonizio

PROMPT: the knot of the self that won't untangle

POEM: Manifesto: The Mad Farmer Liberation Front by Wendell Berry

PROMPT: Write your own manifesto as directives or commands

POEM: Remember by Joy Harjo

PROMPT: I remember

WRITING SAMPLE: written in writing workshop

Scars by Wendy Brown-Baez

I have scars on my hips where the hip replacements were pounded into place. These scars are reminders that I may have once moved effortlessly, dancing and leaping and turning cartwheels with complete joy, and now I don't. They remind me that I am slowing down after a lifetime of walking, hiking, hitchhiking—if I couldn't find a bus or a train, I'd just walk. Proud flesh—how easily I show them off in my bathing suit. And yet there are other scars—the ones on the heart. I can show these off when I feel able and ready but there are moments when I can't believe they are there—when I wish they could be erased. I know we all have scars. They make us who we are. They make us the wearers of proud flesh.

Writing for healing is valuable for participants who have experienced personal trauma from abuse, loss, or incarceration; those experiencing uncertainty from homelessness, dislocation, divorce, or job loss; and those experiencing physical or mental health challenges.

For those participants who are coping with a health crisis, bodily discomfort can interfere with attention; the workshop has to be as easy as possible. I choose poems that are short and read them myself. I may begin by asking each participant to write an affirmation as a way to introduce themselves to the group. I mention the benefits of writing and point out that we are accessing our inner guidance for healing.

The benefits of writing to heal were studied by Dr. James Pennebaker, of the University of Texas at Austin, and Joshua Smyth, PhD, of Syracuse University. Their studies suggest that writing about emotions can boost immune functioning in patients with such illnesses as HIV/AIDS, asthma and arthritis. Intensive research review by Smyth, published in 1998 in the *Journal of Consulting and Clinical Psychology* (Vol. 66, No. 1), notes that writing makes a difference, though the degree of difference depends on the population being studied and the form that writing takes.

Writing that describes a traumatic or distressing event in detail, then pinpoints our feelings at the time and follows with how we feel about it now, is the only kind of writing that has clinically been proven to improve health. Writing can help us understand the past and coach ourselves toward the future but when we access deeper insight, immune function as well as emotional and physical health improves, and behavioral changes occur. Further experiments have demonstrated that months later, better life choices are made and productivity at work or school increased after this method of writing with reflection on the meaning of the distressing event. Chemicals are released in the brain such as dopamine and serotonin, similar to those released during meditation and yoga, giving relief from discomfort and a heightened sense of well-being.

Other studies have shown that people who kept a journal after heart surgery recovered more rapidly than those who did not. They experienced fewer complications and fewer return trips to the doctor. But those who shared their writings in a support group had the greatest benefits. This speaks to how important it is for us to feel heard.

I had the personal experience of writing with a young woman who was too nauseous after chemo to write but asked that we meditate together. In our short meditation we visualized her standing on a bridge. I asked her who was with her on the bridge and what was on the other side. She could only see darkness. When I asked her to imagine someone coming toward her, she visualized a being of light. I guided her through a process of receiving that light and having it pour through her cells. We created a list of affirmations and a list of possible writing prompts. We discussed her recurring negative thoughts and I suggested that she list ways to change them into positive thoughts, both by using mindful techniques such as affirmations and meditation and what I called distractions such as music, phone calls, and audible books. After an hour she said she felt better, and even a little hungry. I believe this was the result of becoming aware of her emotional state and expressing it to another.

The key to writing's effectiveness is in the way people use it to interpret their experiences. Venting emotions alone—whether through writing or talking—is not enough to relieve stress, and thereby improve health, Smyth emphasizes. "To tap writing's healing power, people must use it to better understand and learn from their emotions," he says. Transformation which shows up as a change of attitude, understanding or perspective is the key to using writing to heal effectively. My experience is that this transformation can happen quickly in a group setting as the writer hears his or her own words spoken aloud.

Researchers also found that initial writing about trauma triggers distress and physical and emotional arousal. And "not all people will work through that distress therapeutically or through continued writing," warns psychologist Helen Marlo, PhD, of Notre Dame de Namur University and a private practitioner in Burlingame, California. Smyth's assertion that writing is beneficial according to the way it is used is echoed by health psychology researcher Susan Lutgendorf, PhD, of the University of Iowa. An intensive journaling study conducted with her doctoral student Phil Ullrich suggests that people who relived upsetting events without focusing on meaning reported poorer health than those who derived meaning from the writing. They even fared worse than people who wrote about neutral events. Those who focused on meaning developed greater awareness of the potentially positive aspects of a stressful event.

"You need focused thought as well as emotions," says Lutgendorf. "An individual needs to find meaning in a traumatic memory as well as to feel the related emotions to reap positive benefits from the writing exercise."

I alternate prompts that will bring up difficult emotions and prompts to emphasize our blessings, ways we find joy and pleasure, and ways we take care of ourselves.

More on this topic can be found in Louisa de Salvo's book *Writing as a Way of Healing.*

Receiving the 2012 Minnesota State Arts Board grant enabled me to take writing workshops to twelve non-profit arts and human services organizations. This meant that I was writing in groups sometimes two or three times a week. The surprise gift that I received was my own healing. I wrote with the participants and shared my work, again taking care to direct my work toward the branch of insight, lessons learned, new perspectives discovered or deeper meanings explored. Because I was writing on such a consistent basis, my intuition was guiding me powerfully, both in my writing and in the prompts I chose. I wrote with honesty about my own disappointments, grief, regret, guilt, and heartache. As a workshop leader, I learned to write very quickly and was able to foresee which way my writing might lead me. I could take the road to going deeper into the drama of the story or I could veer to a positive shift of perspective. For the sake of my participants, I choose that shift. This hastened my own healing process.

Interestingly enough, even though I was using some of the same prompts over and over, each time I found a new focus, entry point, emerging details, memories, emotions, shift in perspective or awareness. I seldom wrote the same response to the same prompt twice and usually found gems of insight previously hidden from my conscious awareness.

The turning point came when writing with the heart support group at Abbot Northwestern Hospital. Our prompt was "Grace or luck". I began to write about Michael who had incredible luck: a daredevil who walked away from motorcycle accidents, talked his way out of speeding tickets, was given the best hotel room without a reservation, breaking hearts while staying friends. But as I wrote about how it appeared that my own luck dissolved when he died, I realized how often I had been graced. I shrugged off the burden of "victim" to understand that I had been graced with multiple opportunities such as the grant and teaching, I had found deep friendships and community, and I was moving forward in the direction of my dreams.

Books had been published! Events and readings organized! I looked back and the long hard years of struggle slid away to be replaced by many gifts of support, friendship, and inspiration. This shifted my perspective about the past ten years.

PROMPTS FOR WRITING TO HEAL OR CARE FOR THE SOUL

WARM UPS:

I may not be perfect but I….

Instead of silence

Calling home

What would it take

Live as if

I'm just not ready

After the storm

The moment I knew I was different

5 things I know, 5 things I don't know, 5 things I want to know

gratitude to: one body part, one person, one talent, one memory

POEM: So Much Happiness by Naomi Shihab Nye

PROMPTS: It is difficult to know what to do…

This is what I want you to know…

POEM: Otherwise by Wislawa Szymborska

PROMPTS: it could have been

the direction I am going

what my future self tells me

POEM: Sometimes by David Whyte

PROMPT: What's your "question that won't go away"?

POEM: Sorrows by Lucille Clifton

PROMPT: what holds me back

POEM: Don't allow the lucid moment to dissolve by Adam Zagajewski

PROMPT: what I can't forget

POEM: Ode a la Vida by Pablo Neruda

PROMPT: write your own ode to life

POEM: List of Praises by Anne Porter

PROMPT: praise ordinary blessings and then praise something that is hard to praise: the jewel in the compost, the struggle or the difficulty

POEM: A Blessing by James Wright

PROMPTS: what breaks me into blossom

how a human being can change

POEM: Spent by Mark Doty

PROMPT: second chances

POEM: The Gardener by Ken Weisner

PROMPT: on my knees

POEM: Little Stones at My Window by Mario Benedetti

PROMPT: what gives me joy

POEM: Only One by Denise Levertov

PROMPT: the marvelous in my life

POEM: Testament by Ruth Foley

PROMPT: what legacy do I leave (include objects, memories, abstract qualities of your personality)

POEM: For a New Beginning by John O'Donohue

PROMPT: what I accomplished this year, include small things such as yoga class, keeping a journal, a new outfit, gardening, sitting by the lake, then go on to bigger things

Set intentions for new year

POEM: Nothing Gold Can Stay by Robert Frost

PROMPT: what I need to let go of

POEM: Barter by Sara Teasdell

PROMPT: write about the lovely things in your life, where do you find them

POEM: I Will Not Die an Unlived Life by Dawna Markova

PROMPT: what goes on from you to blossom and bear fruit

POEM: Permissions Granted by David Allen Sullivan

PROMPT: I give myself permission

POEM: Saint Francis and the Sow by Galway Kinnel

PROMPT: how I bless myself

POEM: Last Night as I Was Sleeping by Antonio Machado

PROMPT: how I make honey from my failures

POEM: Prayer in The Strip Mall, Bangor, Maine by Stuart Kestenbaum

PROMPT: random love

POEM: Love After Love by Derek Wolcott

PROMPT: give back my heart, what I want to say to my heart and how my heart responds

POEM: Caretake this moment by Epictetus

PROMPT: I am not alone because….

POEM: Pray with your whole body by Wendy Brown-Baez
Sometimes by Margaret Mitchell
PROMPT: how I pray (with my actions)

POEM: The Journey by David Whyte
PROMPT: What is ending, what is beginning

POEM: Expect Nothing by Alice Walker
PROMPT: I surprise myself

POEM: A Note by Wislawa Szymborska
PROMPT: what pain is not

Writing Exercise:

When I feel sad, I…

When I feel discouraged, I…

When I am in pain, I …

When I feel self-doubt, I …

When I feel fearful, I…

When I feel happy, I …

When I feel energized, I …

When I feel confident, I …

When I feel joy, I …

One small step toward joy would be…

10 Reasons to Live

- include one person, place or thing
- one abstract quality
- one emotional state

RESOURCES

- *Writing as a Way of Healing: How Telling Our Stories Transforms Our Lives* by Louise DeSalvo (Beacon Press, 1999).
- *Poetic Medicine: The Healing Art of Poem Making* by John Fox (Tarcher, 1997)
- *Opening Up: The Healing Power of Expressing Emotions* by James W. Pennebaker (The Guilford Press, 1997).
- *Writing to Heal: A Guided Journal for Recovering from Trauma and Emotional Upheaval* by James Pennebaker (New Harbinger, 2004).
- *Fearless Confessions: A Writers Guide to Memoir* by Sue William Silverman. (The University of Georgia Press, 2009).
- *Maps of Narrative Practice* by Michael White (W. W. Norton & Company, 2007)
- *Writing to Heal the Soul: Transforming Grief and Loss Through Writing* by Susan Zimmermann (Harmony 2002)

WRITING EXERCISE:

Gratitude is a quality that has been proven to uplift, comfort, transform, and heal.

Write a paragraph with gratitude to: one body part, one person, one talent, one memory

_____

_____

_____

_____

_____

_____

_____

_____

_____

_____

_____

_____

_____

_____

_____

_____

_____

_____

_____

_____

_____

_____

RESPONSES FROM PARTICIPANTS IN A WRITING CIRCLES FOR HEALING WORKSHOP:

- Allows me to put into words what I feel without judgement.
- I've learned to express myself.
- Thank you from the bottom of my heart. Uplifting insights on my past and present.
- Temporary escape from stress of chronic illness
- This is such a powerful medium of tuning into self.
- I feel good, relieved, relaxed.
- I am often reticent in a group. I hesitate to speak…I NEVER felt inhibited to scribble and read anything that came to me.
- It was wonderful to let go of the logical and discover who I could be in the moment.
- It helps me get in touch with my inner spirit.
- Helped me process my grief and get in touch with my feelings.
- Probably the most transformative class I've taken yet.
- Today felt sacred.
- The highlight of the session: The authentic tears and laughter through each person's sharing
- Thanks for helping me find myself.
- It made me realize I haven't allowed myself to cry.
- It helped me to live in the present and not be so distracted.
- Reminds me how much benefit I get from stopping and reflecting.
- It gave me a different perspective.
- I realized the quietness in myself delved into a gentle honesty.
- Helped me focus more on healthy things like meditation.
- Gave me time to process.
- I'm an anxious sharer so it's good to be forced to be vulnerable.

- It helped me let go of my perfectionism and get in touch with my intuition and inner capacity for healing.
- Let go of held back feelings.
- It always seems to open up a part of myself.
- Made me want to keep writing for more insight, released feelings that had been repressed from long ago.
- The entire session may be the highlight of my month. It opened up my creativity big time.
- Highlight of the session: sharing and realizing we all have similar experiences.

Victims of Domestic Violence

O ne of the first workshops I taught even before moving permanently to Minnesota was at Cornerstone, a place that provides shelter and support for victims of domestic violence. I was visiting for several months during the birth of my grandson and wanted to try my wings as a writing workshop facilitator. When I spoke to the volunteer coordinator, we decided that I could lead writing exercises during their support group sessions, two sessions each for two different groups. They would have experienced the process at least once and we would be able to build on it in the second session. Often I hear something in someone's writing that triggers the thought of a particular poem or prompt to use the next time.

Part of the process of volunteering for non-profits that provide human services is to fill out an application form, have a background check, and meet with either staff or a committee. If you intend to teach at non-profits, be prepared to spend more time in meetings and emailing or making phone calls than you first anticipated. I found that almost always making the initial contact to propose the class was best accomplished in person. You want to communicate how the class is going and perhaps who attended if staff is not present. The organization might create flyers for you to post in their facility or they might ask for a workshop description.

At Cornerstone, one of the questions on the volunteer application asked whether I had ever been abused. My knee jerk reaction was to say no, but then I had to stop and think while considering the definition of "abuse." Did that include being put down in front of others or negative reactions to my ideas? Did that include my partner disappearing and calling me from another state? Did that include taking risks on the highway by driving too fast even after I asked him to slow down? Did that include demanding I listen to his thoughts about suicide? Before that, was it abuse to be told how to dress, who I could travel with, and how to parent? Was it abuse to be told who could or could not be my boyfriend and the demand of sexual relations whether or not I was feeling attracted to that person? This was a revelation, to consider myself as someone who had been abused. I had something in common with the women I would be writing with, more than I had realized.

The writing was immediately poignant and deep. The women freely allowed their emotions to come onto the page. As often happens, one woman wrote something that she was very excited about sharing. She had written about her life and had found a new perspective—she shouldn't blame herself and realized she must move on. The excitement flew around the circle. We all were uplifted by the feeling of hope and renewal.

I led a workshop at Harriet Tubman which also provides shelter and support for victims of domestic violence. At Harriet Tubman we met in the morning over coffee and doughnuts. Often the caseworker had to go to their rooms to remind participants it was time for the class. In the beginning, we had sporadic attendance but as the women became enthusiastic about what they were writing and discovering about themselves, they spread the word and encouraged others to join us. One of the most noticeable results was that the women started to share their stories with each other and to give each other advice and encouragement. Before the workshop, the shame of being battered prevented them from sharing in an intimate and honest way. They had learned to shut up and now they were opening up.

The participants in a class such as one held at a shelter for victims of domestic violence will be reluctant to participate because they do not feel they are smart enough or are not good writers. In this case, it is essential to start with poems that are easy to understand and to reassure them that there is no right or wrong way to do the process. It helps if the staff is enthusiastic and if the women talk it up amongst themselves. Due to the turmoil of their lives, the necessity to not only remove themselves from an abusive situation, perhaps with someone they care about deeply, and to plan and take action to create a new life, they are under psychological and financial stress and may be suffering from PTSD. Often they have small children and must find childcare or sign up for it if the shelter provides it, and occasionally they will leave the class early to check on their children. I have also encountered a situation where a stipend for the participants to attend was requested. It is important to not have expectations of who will show up, if they will come back, if they will stay, and if they will be willing to share. Over time, as they learn to trust the process, it gets easier.

Often there will be one woman who has been waiting for this opportunity, who has been journaling or writing songs or poems all her life and who is more enthusiastic and ready to open up. I always begin reading after writing by asking who would like to start. This gives the group a feeling of control and ownership of the circle. Then I go around the circle one by one to ask if the next participant wants to share. This gives those who feel shy a chance to share if they are ready to. If the group seems particularly shy about sharing, I will remind them that I want to hear their voices, that this is their opportunity to be heard. As I mentioned in the beginning chapter on process, I do not comment on their writing except to praise something that is especially honest or vulnerable and note when the writing is expressive or descriptive. My comments tend to be about strategies that can help us through tough times. I share ideas for mindful breathing practices, encourage self-expression as a way to break patterns and coach ourselves towards a better future, suggest ways to nourish oneself through healthy choices and praise the recovery of self-worth.

WRITING EXERCISES FOR VICTIMS OF DOMESTIC VIOLENCE

POEM: Courage by Ann Sexton

PROMPT: what gives me courage

POEM: Antilamentation by Dorianne Laux

PROMPTS: If I could change one thing

what I regret, what I don't

POEM: Stone by Charles Simic

PROMPT: what is written on my inner walls

POEM: The Journey by Mary Oliver

PROMPTS: the life I saved

what I had to do

POEM: sorrows by Lucille Clifton

PROMPT: what no one knows about me

POEM: Crossroads by Joyce Stuphen

PROMPT: starting over

POEM: If You Only Knew by Marjorie Bruhmuller

PROMPT: if you only knew

POEM: All the True Vows by David Whyte

PROMPT: something of my own

POEMS: Spent by Mark Doty

Begin by Brendan Kennelly

PROMPT: second chances

POEM: Kindness by Naomi Shihab Nye

PROMPT: what I left behind and what I kept

POEM: So Much Happiness by Naomi Shihab Nye

PROMPT: happiness is….

POEM: I'm Going to Start Living Like a Mystic by Edward Hirsch

PROMPT: I'm going to start living…..

POEM: Sweet Darkness by David Whyte

PROMPT: waking up

POEM: Boats in the Bay by Winifred Holtby

PROMPT: a ritual to get rid of my sorrows

POEM: Lot's Wife by Wislawa Szymborska

PROMPT: looking back

POEM: What Do Women Want by Kim Addonizio

PROMPT: what do you yearn for

POEM: Instructions in Joy by Nancy Shaffer

PROMPT: what brings me joy, gives me hope

SAMPLES OF SELF-REFLECTIVE WRITING:

I include complete samples of writing that I shared because I believe the facilitator must model for the group one's own process and discoveries. Not only is it essential to be vulnerable and honest on the page and willing to share, but to demonstrate your own process of finding meaning. It is important for the participants to hear affirmations of courage and strength in your work. Sometimes you will hear the participants write something that is affirming or you can lead them to write positive affirmations, then suggest that they print them out and tape them somewhere they will see every day. Praise is important, as they have heard negative, wounding remarks from their partners and their sense of self-esteem has been damaged. Whenever you can, point out their courage and share your admiration for their determination to create a new life.

What I had to do

was pack my bags and don't look back. But I am a writer, so of course I look back, constantly it seems. A trail of little pebbles of regret. And yet I kept moving, leaps of faith that my wings will grow. What I had to do was admit that I am worth it. I had to not only admit it but act on it. I had to pack my belief in myself in that suitcase I brought along with me and then take it out, shake out the wrinkles and the creases. What I had to do was to learn my own value in the love I felt but also in setting boundaries—it was in the forgiveness but also in the ability to say enough—it was in the dreams I had put aside and needed to pick up again. I had to pack up all those dreams and take them with me and at the next turn of the spiral, when I had caught my breath, unpack them and hang them in my own space. It didn't matter that the space was borrowed. I made it made it mine as soon as I unpacked my memories, my dreams, and my belief that I was worth it. What I had to do was stop and ask for help. To realize that the direction I was going was not the direction I had to stay in. I could turn around and find true north.

What gets in my way

is myself—comparisons, frustration because I think I need to do more, be more, impatience at how long it has taken to get here, discouragement at how far I need to go. Perfection is a hope, a dream and an illusion, says the Recovery Inc aphorism. And surely I know by now I am perfect exactly as I am, with my scars and my loves and my tears and my passions.

Try to love the obstacles, the lessons they bring, courage to take the risk, determination not to give up, hope that the transformation that is happening will pull me through, out of the mush of the chrysalis to spread my wings. What gets in my way is limited perception instead of unlimited vision. To look back with gratitude and see how closely I walked on the edge due to some inner imperative to risk myself—to see how often I have received support, guidance, love— to understand that whatever I need to do, I am doing.

To be joyful it the present moment as a choice until it becomes a way of being—this is my daily task. To surrender to the good is sometimes harder than struggling against the negative but I am surely on the pilgrim's path to the blessing, arriving where I belong and where I will not falter longer than a heartbeat.

What I am stripping off

is regret and guilt and all the ways the past didn't turn out the way I expected.

Complaint without answer. Find heaven in this moment instead.

What I am putting on is joy and confidence and visions of the future. Not yearning but blessings and being blest. Not restless but rested and focused. Not wanderer or pilgrim. Not lonely but solitary.

What I am stripping off is the messages that I can't have it all, can't be woman and clever or wise and youthfully playful. What I am putting on is the majestic robes of wisdom earned and the pearls of great price I dug out of the compost.

What I am stripping off is that it requires hard work and struggle, loneliness and sacrifice. I am putting on ease, as the wind blowing through the trees, river over rocks, flowers blooming in a field. I am stripping off the layers of paint to reveal the wood underneath, solid heart of the tree. I am putting on the grace I found had been in my closet all along.

What I know about love

is that it is a coming home to yourself. It is a knowing. That the more we practice it, the wider the heart stretches. That the beauty we love is not only the way we kneel and kiss the ground but also the way our wings shake themselves out of our shoulders. What I know about love is that it is a gift and a grace and it flows from the earth, a rhythm that matches out heart beat and our breath. It flows from the things of this earth, the living proof that creation is a miracle, the tangible proof that we are here for joy. What I know about love is that I often looked for it in all the wrong places and for all the wrong reasons. I mistook need for desire and desire for purpose. I thought if I gave enough away I would never be abandoned, I wouldn't be alone. But now I understand that love is my way of enfolding the world to myself, to keep me warm, to keep me entertained, to keep me lit up, a small lantern against the dark. What I know about love is that it is a surprise and yet a recognition. Oh here you are, and here I am, arms opened to a song that sings me alive.

Story as Medicine

In an interview in Radiance Magazine, Clarissa Pinkoles Estes said: "In this tradition a story is 'holy,' and it is used as medicine. The story is not told to lift you up, to make you feel better, or to entertain you, although all those things can be true. The story is meant to take the spirit into a descent to find something that is lost or missing and to bring it back to consciousness again." This is a perfect description of writing through grief, to descend into emotional darkness in order to find secret blessings and bring them consciously into our lives.

I often begin a writing circle by sharing my own story in order to create intimacy. The story is adjusted according to the group. For Story as Medicine, I share how death of loved ones impacted my writing.

In Santa Fe, I was invited to join a women's poetry group hosted by Marcia Starck, a renowned astrologer and community activist for social justice. We eventually were five women, woven together by the threads of social activism and storytelling. I was writing in a group setting twice a week. During the increasing pressure of Michael's illness on me, I had a creative out-let as my words poured onto the page and were shared for support, feedback and encouragement. After his death, a burst of creative energy forged my identity as a poet.

The women's group decided to hold our first public reading at a coffeehouse during *Día de los Muertos,* Day of the Dead, to honor those we had lost, incorporating ritual, dramatic gesture and costume. After hours of brainstorming, we named ourselves Word Dancers. We were a group of dramatic women: a storyteller, actresses, and theater director, so we knew we wanted to give a performance that would be more theatrical than just reading poems one after the other. We decided we would do "rounds" or specific topics and have each of us read a poem that fit the topic. The order we would read would depend on the flow between poems. We decided that we would have one humorous round, one round about social justice, and one round about personal loss.

A poem had come to me the day before Michael died that I wanted to share but felt too intimate and emotional to read it from a piece of paper. I needed the audience to embrace me and support me, so I memorized it. The connection was so electrifying and gratifying that I decided to memorize all of my poetry. I became a performance poet and traveled to the East Coast and West Coast, created personas and rituals for my work, and released a poetry CD. Some of my poems were published. I was energized, inspired and finally doing what I loved to do.

Michael's death was an initiation, but it did not prepare me for the shocking death of my son three years later. In the summer of 2005 while visiting Minneapolis, my youngest son Sam committed suicide. I had finally healed from Michael's death and it felt as though the rug was pulled out from under me; my life totally shattered. Disorientated, engulfed in deep anger, my world tipped out of balance. I could not pray or meditate or write. I returned to Santa Fe and eventually re-joined my writing groups. I figured that even though I could not write, I could show up and listen. These were my friends, this was my routine. Once the pen was in my hand, however, it was natural to put it to paper. Like riding a bicycle, the habit of writing came back, because it was a habit I had established over time.

Alejandro Báez and I had married in 2004 in order to continue his medical care. He returned to Mexico in October 2005 and the following spring, I moved to Puerto Vallarta. Together we opened Sol y Luna art gallery. To honor mourning within the context of community, I created a bilingual *Día de los Muertos* performance with a local man enlisted as my co-performer.

Day of the Dead is one of the most cherished traditions of the Mexican people. The Mexicans are fatalistic although they also poke fun at death, as if to remove the sting. It is both a reverent and festive time.

One poem I performed was *La Coqueta* by E. A. Mares. It begins by listing names for Lady Death: the Stinky One, the Bony One, the Hag, the Bitch, the Fucked Up, as well as the more traditional La Catrina and Doña Sebastiana. The poem is about near-fatalities. My co-performer and I called these names out to each other across the audience as if we were enticing Lady Death to come near. Suddenly I had the revelation that death comes to all, that we have each suffered a death, or will, and that we each will die. I asked the audience to light a candle in honor of a deceased loved one. As I looked out over the sea of flames, the realization surged through me that Death is a part of life, a part of the cycle of life-death-regeneration. It marked a turning point in my healing.

When leading a group in writing through grief, I use ritual as a container for the writing process. We each light a candle and name who or what we are grieving. Rather than focus on the grief itself, I focus on the way it impacts us: what traits we may have inherited, what gifts or blessings or new insight we gained during this time, how we have changed, how we are transformed and deepened. I talk about death as an initiation, as a liminal space where we encounter the invisible world in-between, and the importance of ritual. We can feel disoriented, extra-sensitive, and deeply intuitive. I share the traditions of *Día de los Muertos*, how the entire Mexican community celebrates and honors their dead. We discuss how we are not able to grieve the way we need to in our society but rather are encouraged to get on with our lives as quickly as possible.

I prefer to have at least three sessions to take us through the process, to take us into the depths that Estes speaks of and be uplifted at the end. We conclude each session by blowing out the candles. At the first session I ask that they say a blessing to the person or grief they named and to let go if they are able. For the second session we express gratitude for the lesson or insights earned. At the third session we bless ourselves.

During this last session we share any tributes we have written to our loved ones. In the first workshop I led, participants wrote about grief over divorce, job and home loss so our tributes were to our own gifts and strengths. The second workshop focused on loss of a loved one. Everyone was invited to bring a symbolic object to represent the loved one for our last session and place it on the altar. We stood together in front of the altar as we shared what we had written and sang together before blowing out the candles.

It is essential to write with the group and share your writing so that everyone feels you are equally invested. At the same time, it is imperative to lead and not be so emotional that the group must take care of you. This requires allowing emotions to surface while remaining in control and aware of the group dynamic. The position of leadership requires engagement and strength. If you have unresolved grief, it may be necessary to undergo your own counseling before you lead a group. Deep emotions rise to the surface and tears are easily shed. If the group feels bonded, other members of the group will reach out to each other, offering Kleenex, consolations, and comfort. It is up to you to determine when it is time to be silent, when it is time to move on, and when it is time to read something uplifting. The workshop ends with a positive affirmation of life and confirmation that life goes on, that we are reborn.

At the end of the workshop, shake out the energy by standing and literally shaking, stretching, or moving in a physical way. Often I ask participants to place a hand on their hearts and thank themselves for showing up.

WRITING WORKSHOP FOR LOSS & GRIEF

1st session: What I lost and what I was able to keep

PROMPTS:

first memory

what I love about you

what I inherited from you

writing a letter to you: what I never got to say

POEMS:

Trying to Raise the Dead by Dorianne Laux

Self-portrait by David Whyte

Nothing Gold Can Stay by Robert Frost

Horses by Kate Dicamillo

Dirge Without Music by Edna St. Vincent Millay

2nd session: What I can't take back: regret

What part of me did I lose? What did I gain?

PROMPTS:

good memories, difficult memories

the last words you said to me

what I yearn for

the blessing in the difficulty

POEMS:

For What Binds Us by Jane Hirschfield

She said by Daniel Forest

For My Grandmother's Perfume, Norell by Nickole Brown

In Heaven It is Always Autumn by Elizabeth Spires

3rd session: Blessings and gifts

PROMPTS:

what gives me strength

what no one knows

I'm going to start living…..

POEMS:

I'm Going to Start Living Like a Mystic by Edward Hirsch

Sweetness by Stephen Dunn

In the Kirkegaard, December by Athena Kildegaard

4th session: How did grief change me

How am I rebirthed?

PROMPTS:

who am I now

when we meet again

at the edge of the holy

and still I rise

POEMS:

Praise What Comes by Jeanne Lohman

I will not live an unlived life by Dawna Markova

Lying in Wait for Happiness by Yehuda Amichai

Grief Comes with a Ladder by Richard Solly

Grief by Wendy Brown-Baez

ADDITIONAL MATERIAL:

excerpt from *Soul Mates* by Thomas Moore The Future of Former Relationships pg 200-203

excerpt from *Women Who Run with the Wolves* by Clarissa Pinkoles Estes: Battle Scars: Membership in the Scar Clan pg 285

Excerpt from *A Grief Observed* by C. S. Lewis: "No one ever told me that grief felt so like fear. I am not afraid, but the sensation is like being afraid. The same fluttering in the stomach, the same restlessness, the yawning. I keep on swallowing.

At other times it feels like being mildly drunk, or concussed. There is a sort of invisible blanket between the world and me. I find it hard to take in what anyone says. Or perhaps, hard to want to take it in. It is so uninteresting. Yet I want the others to be about me. I dread the moments when the house is empty. If only they would talk to one another and not to me."

BOOK RESOURCES:

The Art of Losing: Poems of Grief and Healing edited by Kevin Young, Bloomsbury

Beloved on the Earth: 150 Poems of Grief and Gratitude edited by Jim Perlman, Deborah Cooper, Mara Hart and Pamela Mittlefehldt, Holy Cow! Press

The Wind Blows, the Ice Breaks: Poems of Loss and Renewal by Minnesota Poets edited by Ted Bowman and Elizabeth Bourque Johnson, Nodin Press

The Wild Edges of Sorrow, Rituals of Renewal and the Sacred Work of Grief by Francis Weller, North Atlantic Books

WRITING SAMPLES

What I lost by Wendy Brown-Baez

> What I lost is the conversation and the presence, watching my son grown up and the pride I felt as a mother. I lost the definition of myself, the identity of a loving mother. I should have known and was puzzled that I didn't—hadn't intuited—and that part of myself that is true, intuitive knowing, felt broken and bruised, I stopped trusting myself, What I lost was the bright colors and spices of New Mexico because I couldn't stay, the limpid lazy beach in Mexico because I

couldn't stay. The ability to live by myself and to love solitude. It felt like I lost everything at first, but I never completely lost myself.

The blessing from grief by Wendy Brown-Baez

The blessing I received from grief was taking off my rose-colored glasses and seeing things as they really are. The blessing is knowing my own strength and endurance to keep going, to know what to do in order to celebrate and honor my loved one, when it was okay to cry and when it was okay to lead others toward their own silence or stories. The blessing was my friendships, those who stood by me and the outpouring of love. The blessing was rituals and how they soothed the worst part of the pain. Going to the monastery for Thanksgiving and allowing myself to be enfolded into a spiritual community amongst the majestic beauty of the Chama River canyon. Sitting in church before candles lit to Guadalupe and letting my heart crack open. The blessing was becoming authentic—becoming more true to my own self and my passions and finding the courage to follow my dreams. Letting go was hard and yet, it gave me the lift-off to get out of a place that could have become a rut to expand. Letting go of my resistance to change. The blessing was staying in the possibility of gratitude despite anger, guilt, grief, regret. The dark night of the soul required finding the small eternal flame within myself, not just words or belief but a deep inner knowing. Being able to hear the deep grief of others, and understanding the blessing was that moment of connection, knowing that I have been where you are. The blessing is that I learned life goes on in ways I had never dreamed possible.

Write what you lost and what you were able to keep.

_____

_____

_____

_____

_____

_____

_____

_____

_____

Write about the unexpected blessings of grief

_____

_____

_____

_____

_____

_____

_____

_____

_____

_____

_____

_____

_____

The Aliveness Project

My passion for words has resulted in two large plastic boxes stuffed with journals, hundreds of unpublished pages, dozens of notebooks filled with scribbles, and files bulging with advice for writers. I finally created that writer's life I dreamed of when I began to bring writing for healing workshops to non-profit organizations, schools for at risk youth, healing centers, the prison and women's retreats. The purpose of the workshops is to access one's intuition and allow the story you are compelled to tell to rise to the surface.

The change from creative writing to writing for healing came to me after the loss of my son Sam. After the worst of the despair and grieving had passed, I realized that I had a passion for words and language, I had the wisdom of experience, and I wanted to be of service. They say we teach what we need to learn. My own healing would take years of counseling, detours to Mexico and poetry performances on *Día de los Muertos*, retreats, healing circles, spending time with grandsons, spiritual community, and my own writing practice. Writing in groups propelled me forward to both tell my story and to reconsider it from the angle of what it might mean, what I have learned, and what gifts I have received even through tragedy.

One of the first workshops I taught as a volunteer was at The Aliveness Project. The Aliveness Project is a non-profit resource for people who are HIV positive. They provide a hot meal and bags of groceries, counseling, massages, and stress management classes.

I wrote with a group of men, many of whom had never written anything before. In fact, during our check in, one confided that he hated writing ever since elementary school. Due to the funding constraints of their programming, we were only able to meet twice but the writing was powerful. At the second session, one man shared that he has been part of a support group for 6 months but had never formally introduced himself to the group. "This past meeting, I read what I wrote in class as a way to introduce myself," he said. This brought tears to my eyes.

In this class, not only did we have inexperienced writers but I had to quickly create a sense of trust and intimacy. The men had to trust that I would not judge them, their lifestyle, their choices or the ways they coped. It was fortunate that I was able to share that I had been married to a man who was HIV+ and that I understood the daily task of staying optimistic and taking care of oneself. With this level of vulnerability, it is especially important to write with the group and share one's writings. As facilitators, it is important to remember that it is up to us to uplift the group no matter how deeply we go and how many tears are shed. We must have a writing habit that enables us to take the path of finding the meaning, the lesson learned, the beauty and mystery inherent in all of life, the possibilities of healing, the resolution or understanding, and end the session with something positive, funny or kind. Sometimes this means including a small detail of daily life, something I noticed that is unique or beautiful, or making fun at myself, such as admitting that my favorite part of yoga is the rest pose at the end.

WRITING EXERCISES FOR HIV+ CLIENTS

WARM UP: What will it take?

On the edge

I knew I was in trouble when

Calling home

POEM: The Winter of Listening by David Whyte

PROMPT: live as if

POEM: Praise for the Ordinary Day by Wendy Brown-Baez

PROMPT: the hardest thing to do

POEM: Why I Love Mornings by Nancy Boutilier

PROMPT: a fresh start

POEM: Stone by Charles Simic

PROMPT: what is written on your inner walls

POEM: Crying Poem by Jimmy Santiago Baca

PROMPT: what I regret and what I don't regret

what my tears tell me

POEM: whose side are you on? by Lucille Clifton

PROMPT: standing up for myself

POEM: I am Going to Start Living Like a Mystic by Edward Hirsch

PROMPT: I am going to start living like...

POEM: The Journey by David Whyte

PROMPT: what is written in the ashes of your life

We also used some of the poems and prompt ideas from the previous writing for healing chapter.

The writing was powerful and life-affirming. Often in a circle, you hear what you wish you had written, because you feel the same way or what you wish you had thought of, because you recognize yourself.

WRITING SAMPLE: How I stand up for myself by Wendy Brown-Baez

I stand up for myself by speaking my truth aloud. I stand up for myself by being true to myself and not changing to fit someone else's image. By looking for the blessing, finding the good, the jewel in the compost. I stand up for myself by not accepting less than I am worth, even if it means opportunities lost and sometimes I stand up for myself by giving freely. I stand up for myself by accepting myself with my flaws and my failures and by acknowledging my strengths and my success. I stand up for myself by blooming every chance I get.

A few years later, I was able to lead writing workshops again at The Aliveness Project due to a grant received by Patrick's Cabaret. Once again I was struck by the resiliency of the participants. One man wrote about how he was told he had only a few weeks left to live—45 years ago! We burst into cheers and applause. Tears and laughter are a sign to me that the process is working but after our first session, several men told me they were on their way to a funeral. The writing workshop gave me the strength to attend, one man confided as we dispersed.

Writing with Youth in Crisis: In the Shelter of Words project

My first foray into the world of teens in the Twin Cities was when I became the recipient of a McKnight grant through COMPAS Community Action Program. The grant enabled me to teach a writing/performance class at El Colegio High School, a charter school for students who had not been able to graduate due to language barriers, poor academic performance or behavioral issues. My interest in teens came from the time I spent with run-away kids on the streets of Seattle. The contrast between the daily hustle—how to get money and how to stay safe—and their vitality and resiliency had invigorated me at that time.

The COMPAS grant enabled me to approach El Colegio with a specific project. We studied Spanish poets such as Pablo Neruda, Miguel Hernandez and Antonio Machado, wrote together, translated our English poems into Spanish or our Spanish poems into English, and created a performance piece. We wanted to perform the show for the entire school and invite another school to attend our reading as a way to build community.

Unfortunately this project had a lot of bumps and detours. The school itself was dealing with extreme behavior issues and I was told they couldn't hold an assembly of the entire student body. The students who signed up for a performance class became shy at the time of rehearsals.

I counted it as a success when one Spanish-speaking student wrote about being misunderstood because of his imperfect English skills based on the prompt "what makes me angry, what makes me sad and what makes me happy." The other students said they didn't realize that was how he felt and were apologetic. It opened their eyes toward this student and others not fluent in English.

Later, I wanted to volunteer my time with another organization based on providing services to young people. Face to Face offers a free health and wellness clinic to teens and runs SafeZone, a place for homeless teens to have a meal, take a shower, receive counseling, use the computer for job searching, and just hang out.

At SafeZone, the writing group met in the kitchen. Although sporadically attended, when the teens wrote of their challenges, I was amazed at their resiliency. I was especially impressed by the lack of bitterness or blame and their hope and determination to get situated, find work and stabilize.

I used the same technique of spontaneous free writing based on prompts that come from a line, an image or a concept in a poem or from something I heard from them. The teens appreciated and enjoyed the poems but they were particularly interested in sharing their own words and the poems they had been writing.

One of the agreements I had to make as a volunteer was not to greet the teens on the street unless they acknowledged me first, in order to respect their privacy. This started me thinking. I wanted to give teens a voice and draw attention to the issue of teen homelessness. I was flabbergasted to discover the number of homeless teens in the TC area.

The idea of *In the Shelter of Words* began when I started to imagine a portable temporary shelter as place where teen voices could be heard on a CD rather than in-person performance. I imagined a structure similar to the *sukkah*, built by Jewish families after the High Holy Days to remind the Jewish people of the time they lived in tents while crossing the wilderness. In the *sukkah*, everyone is treated equally; in Israel you can visit the prime minister or famous writers in their *sukkahs*. The *sukkah* is traditionally made from found materials. Starlight should be seen through the roof and it is allowed to decompose back into the earth after the holiday is over.

Our structure would represent the transitory nature of the daily lives of teens in crisis as well as a safe place to express their thoughts and feelings, to create a bridge between the participants and the wider community and to create a dialogue about youth in poverty. Our shelter was built by the students of Face to Face Academy with the intention to install it in several community centers throughout the fall and winter. Inside, two chairs, a stereo loaded with the CD, and a bookshelf filled the space. A notebook held written copies of the poems recorded on the CD. *In the Shelter of Words* was installed in the high school for their peers, families, and staff to experience. In April 2012, the art installation began placement in community venues: an art gallery, at a church-sponsored event on homelessness, and at Mid-town Global Market, in order to create awareness of the challenges of homelessness, poverty, abuse, neglect, loss of family and identity, cultural diversity, and the courage of young people in facing those challenges.

In writing with teens I noticed that three minutes of spontaneous writing seemed to be a long time. Sometimes they wanted to dash something off and then leave. To get them to delve deeper into their thoughts and feelings requires patience and repetition but most of all, they must feel they can trust you and the environment. It is essential that each student understands the code of confidentiality for the group and agrees to it. It is also necessary to repeat instructions several times, especially if you are requiring homework or make up work if they are receiving credit.

When working with the youth at The Bridge, a place for teens in transitional housing, the writing workshop was mandatory and their reluctance to be there made it hard to catch their attention. I reminded them that we wanted to hear their voices and as others shared their honest and personal work, they gradually opened up and began to enjoy the class.

One hour is too short; it takes at least half an hour to warm up. On the other hand, after about an hour and a half, they become restless.

In my workshops, I always ask who wants to start, then go around the circle. I have found that this helps participants who are reluctant to share to have more confidence if it is perceived as just their turn rather than offering to read. I also remind the circle that we are only making positive, supportive comments, until we come to the critiquing session which will be included if the students are working toward reading or publishing their work. Writing with teens, this reminder may have to be consistently enforced. Occasionally participants are used to the "popcorn" form of sharing and will read whenever they feel moved to and then I will ask each student who has not read yet if he or she is willing to share. If the students are receiving credit, I tell them that they can pass once in the beginning but after that, they have to share in order to get credit. My experience is that after the initial shyness after the writing exercise, they want to share and feel relieved and uplifted when they do. However, there are times when participants are especially reluctant to write about their feelings, such as when those feelings seem overwhelming, and especially to share them aloud. I started to incorporate a writing exercise in the beginning that would not be shared, such as writing a letter to someone to whom you never got to say the things you wanted to say and putting it in an envelope. I suggested that they burn it, bury it or put it somewhere special. I also have used the prompt "What no one knows about me." One class was particularly reluctant to write about their feelings and we spent one class listing the various ways you can describe a feeling, such as sad/unhappy/bereaved/depressed/ or despondent/sorrowful/heart-broken/melancholy and ways that writing can show the nuances through body language, setting, descriptions, dialogue and inner thoughts. Later I made a presentation in order to interest students in the next semester's creative writing class and asked students what topic they wanted to write about. Half of them wrote "my story."

RESOURCES:

How to Eat a Poem edited by The American Poetry & Literacy Project and The Academy of American Poets (Dover, 2006)

Writing with At-Risk Youth: The Pongo Teen Writing Method by Richard Gold (Rowman & Littlefield, 2014)

WRITING WORKSHOP EXERCISES FOR YOUTH

POEM: Ode to Tortillas by Fernando Esteban Flores

PROMPT: a favorite family meal or holiday

POEM: Blood by Naomi Shihab Nye

PROMPTS: where I come from

my blood, my roots, my family

POEM: My Papa's Waltz by Theodore Roethke

PROMPTS: advice from my grandmother/grandfather/mother/father

What my grandmother told me

POEM: Why I Am Not a Buddhist by Molly Peacock

PROMPT: think about what you are not and would like to be: a football player, a dancer, a journalist, president, a teacher, a poet, a rock star, a rock climber, a scuba diver, a graphic designer

think about what you are not and would not like to be: same as above

think about why you are not: for example, I am not a football player because I don't like to be tackled but then use your imagination to be silly and imaginative such as I am not a football player because I could never be on the field on Sundays. Sundays is when I like to ....

POEM: I Give You Back by Joy Harjo

PROMPT: I give you back (pick a quality: fear, anger, loneliness, sorrow, jealousy, worry, greed, laziness)

Write about how that quality makes you feel and why you give it back. Be incantatory like Joy Harjo's poem, repeat I give you back _____, I give you back because _____

POEM: Kindness by Naomi Shihab Nye

PROMPTS: What I left behind and what I was able to keep

Write about a time when you experienced an unexpected kindness or you were kind

POEMS: Deciding to Stay by Mary Kay Rommel

I Belong There by Darwish Mahmud

I was not born here by Elaine Upton

PROMPT: where I belong

POEM: Wild Geese by Mary Oliver

PROMPT: what will you do with your wild and precious life, what are your dreams and goals

POEM: A Glass of Water by May Sarton

PROMPT: describe yourself doing an ordinary task and then something unexpected happens

POEM: Courage by Anne Sexton

PROMPT: what gives you courage

POEM: My Grandmother in the Stars by Naomi Shihab Nye

PROMPT: where I feel safe

POEMS: Any Case by Wislawa Szymborska

Otherwise by Jane Kenyon

PROMPTS: what if or if only ….if things had been different

If I could change one thing

POEM: Nothing Gold Can Stay by Robert Frost

PROMPT: What is the gold of your life? Will it change?

POEM: Acquainted with the Night by Robert Frost

PROMPTS: I am acquainted with….

what makes you angry, sad, happy?

POEM: A Blessing by James Wright

PROMPTS: What are your blessings?

How do you "burst into blossom"?

POEM: sorrows by Lucille Clifton

PROMPT: What are your sorrows? Your joys?

POEM: whose side are you on? by Lucille Clifton

PROMPTS: Whose side are you on? What would you do if you saw someone
being mistreated/bullied/unjustly judged? Is it okay to take sides?

POEM: Lullaby to the Onion by Miguel Hernandez

PROMPT: When life is hard, how do I find a song to sing?

POEM: Cuando Dormía, Last Night as I was Sleeping by Antonio Machado

PROMPT: How do you make honey out of failure?

POEM: Horses at Midnight Without a Moon by Jack Gilbert

Let's talk about sensual details: use your senses of touch, sight, taste, smell,
sound and feelings

sight: dark/light, colors. textures, weather, distances, space: describe the space you are in

sound: loud/quiet, melodious/harsh, strange/familiar, specific sound such as car horn blasting, rap music pounding, drum beat, heartbeat, breath, rattle of spoons in a drawer, coins in a pocket

touch: hard/soft, rough/ smooth, gentle/rough, hot/cold

taste: sour/sweet, bitter/spicy, specific flavors such as hot chocolate, garlic, crunchy sour apple

smell: sweet/ stinky, fragrant/pungent, zesty, flowery (specific flower), spicy (specific spice)

Feelings: love-anger-surprise-worry-fear-happy-sad-excited-awed-deter-mined-annoyed-inspired

PROMPT: Write a story beginning with a sense detail: the smell of the room as you walk in, the sounds you hear, the quality of the light whether bright sunlight or gloomy or lit by lamps or light and shadows, or the colors and textures

PROMPT: new beginnings

POEM: Winter Thanks by Marcus Jackson

An Ode is a lyrical poem of praise to a person or thing

Write a poem of praise of the natural world. Use your senses to describe the environment: sounds, smells, light/ shadow, and your feelings. Are you excited, scared, awed, annoyed, uplifted, or calm? Use the imagery of the natural world to show your feelings: for example, excited as the chipmunk scampering to gather nuts or excited as the sparking fire, uplifted as the expanse of stars, peaceful as the woodpile?

Include praise to something you normally don't like: spiders or snakes, hard ground or damp morning.

PROMPT: You can start like this: Praise the forest.......praise the meadow.... praise the lake

POEM: Ode to the Onion by Pablo Neruda

PROMPT: write an ode to a common object: your bag, your backpack, iPhone, iPod, your pen, your sweater, your hat, your socks, etc

POEMS: Those Winter Sundays by Robert Hayden

The Gift by Li-Young Lee

PROMPT: my father

POEM: Why I Love Mornings by Nancy Boutilier

PROMPT: what I love

POEM: Twenty Questions by Jim Moore

PROMPT: Write a list of questions and make them into a poem. Is there a thread? Can one question lead to the next? Can you answer the last one?

POEM: Automatic Teller Machine by Ben Mirov

PROMPTS: Are there times when you feel your fate is already decided? How can you change it?

I promise myself

POEM: Stone by Charles Simic

PROMPT: what is written inside of you on your inner walls

POEM: Alice at Seventeen: Like a Wild Child by Darcy Cummings

PROMPT: underneath my skin

POEMS: the topic of gratitude

ODES by Neruda

Gracias a la Vida by Violetta Parra

Alabanza by Martin Espada

Act of Gratitude by Francesc Parcerisas

PROMPT: How do you find the blessing in difficulty?

POEM: How to Own Land by Morgan Farley

PROMPTS: something of my own

How did I get here?

POEM: The Traveling Onion by Naomi Shihab Nye

PROMPT: my kitchen

ADDITIONAL PROMPT IDEAS:

Write a letter to someone you look up to

Dear Mr. President: If I could change things, I would……

We met at the Burger King

Parody of 13 Ways of Looking at a Blackbird: 13 ways of looking at……………

What I dream of

What no one knows about me

This is what I wish I had said

This is what I wish I had not said

My mother/father/grandmother/grandfather's advice

Choices I made

Last night in my neighborhood

Is it okay to be in a gang?

Have you ever had to tell a lie?

My future self tells me…..

To use this as a line and response poem: make a space between lines for students to write a response to the previous line.

Upon Discovering My Entire Solution to the Attainment of Immortality Erased from the Blackboard Except the Word 'Save'

by Dobby Gibson

If you have seen the snow

_____

somewhere slowly fall

_____

on a bicycle,

_____

then you understand

_____

all beauty will be lost

_____

and that even the loss

_____

can be beautiful.

_____

And if you have looked

_____

at a winter garden

_____

and seen not a winter garden

_____

but a meditation on shape,

_____

then you know why

this season is not

known for its words,

the cold too much

about the slowing of matter,

not enough about the making of it.

So you are blessed

to forget this way:

a jump rope in the ice melt,

a mitten that has lost its hand,

a sun that shines

as if it doesn't mean it.

And if in another season

you see a beautiful woman

_____

use her bare hands

_____

to smooth wrinkles

_____

from her expensive dress

_____

for the sake of dignity,

_____

but in so doing trace

_____

the outlines of her thighs,

_____

then you will remember

_____

surprise assumes a space

_____

that has first been forgotten,

_____

especially here, where we

_____

rarely speak of it,

_____

where we walk out onto the roofs

_____

of frozen lakes

---

simply because we're stunned

---

we really can.

Famous Kisses

If I had to choose between kissing Marilyn Monroe

or Einstein I would be stumped. I'd pick Marilyn of course

for her lips had the attention of America, had that much charge

and Joe DiMaggio's home run in them. Arthur Miller's last

line, and they kissed Clark Cable and felt his moustache.

I know that Marilyn tasted of purple conversation hearts,

those packets of candy with slang you buy for Valentine's

and the purple like her lipstick, a little bitter.

Einstein is meanwhile tapping me on the shoulder, whispering

"Space is love" in my left ear. But, Marilyn has me now

with her one shoe dangling from her toe and the eternal

subway grate blowing up under her dress and her legs also

part of the way she kisses. I'm melting at Marilyn's moist

overture, her apertures like Nikon cameras in dim light,

wide open. Kissing Marilyn is American as a California

morning. It's reels of film in silver cans that only live

for screens. Light breaks out, peace breaks out, death

breaks me open and I'm kissing Marilyn Monroe to learn to be

the best kisser in America. But then Einstein gets my

attention. He tickles me with his white erotic hair.

Hair with the energy of atom, of microwave. I can feel

him through my clothes. And for one minute, I turn from

the perfect mammal to the man of mind over matter. I lean

over to him. He kisses me on the cheek. I become younger.

I love backwards. My heart is a ten year old's and I'm

traveling, through space into a perfect equation of love.

--Joan Logghe

PROMPT: I would rather be.......think of a well-known personality or some-one you look up to and admire, why would you like to be like this person?

_____

_____

_____

_____

_____

_____

_____

_____

_____

_____

Unexpected Consequences: writing with teens

This is a true story. It is a story about a dream come true, working with young people, expectations and perfectionism. Leaving room for magic.

As the after-school writing instructor at Face to Face Academy Charter High School, I learned to not take anything for granted. These students were at this small charter school because they wanted to graduate but have fallen behind in traditional school settings for a variety of reasons. Some students had bad luck or made bad choices. Some were parents, some were homeless, some had mental illness or addiction problems, some came from families where English is not the first language at home. Some lived in neighborhoods where police sirens split the night. Some worked.

The students who took the writing workshop are hardworking and mature. Those who weren't serious about doing the work usually tried it for a session, then didn't show up again. Occasionally a pregnant young woman couldn't concentrate or went into labor before the class was completed. Occasionally students returned semester after semester to give it yet another try but dropped out after two sessions when they realized what was expected.

Although it was an after-school program and there was no grading, I assigned homework (it could be completed during the school day and I made it easier each time I gave it yet another try) because that was part of the requirement to keep their charter school status. It was an attempt to weave a thread of additional reading into their lives. When I asked them what they were reading, they shrugged. Texting had replaced reading.

I also was very strict about showing up on time, reading aloud what we write, and turning in a typed piece of prose or poetry on time.

We took turns reading through each poem. Their reading comprehension skills were low and their attention spans short. We discussed vocabulary they did not know and concepts of structure, metaphor and imagery, using our senses and paying attention to the world around us. But mostly we wrote from our personal experiences. What you love and what makes you mad, describe your home and neighborhood, did anything ever happen that you felt was wrong, what did you do or not do about it, if you were the president what would you do? What if you were a journalist or a movie star or a poet or a dream?

I was given an extraordinary opportunity by Saint Paul Almanac, a community-based literary organization that produced a book filled with poems, stories and artwork about Saint Paul. Each month on a Monday night, a reading took place at Black Dog Cafe and I was invited to curate one. I instantly thought of how cool it would be to have my students read, to create a presentation using their work and some of the poems we had studied in class. Best of all, they would get paid for appearing, one of the ways to get young people to show up.

We wrote material that took my breath away in its honesty and wisdom, but they did not want to read those highly personal pieces. That was fine, I let them choose. I asked the English teacher Jennifer if she wanted to share a piece. I was excited about the way our voices would weave together. We started with ten students. Two dropped out, one had her baby, one graduated and moved, and one couldn't get reliable childcare. In the end, we were six females and one male.

We finished the workshop and I came back to the school to rehearse, answering question after question about the reading. I have it all on paper, I assured them. Your poems are in order in a notebook and I have printed out a program to follow.

Then we had Christmas break.

We had agreed to meet at the Black Dog Café a week before the performance to get familiar with the space and practice getting on and off the stage. Mikey and Mai had graduated the previous month so it wasn't too surprising that Jennifer had trouble getting them to commit. But when they told her over the phone that they would *try* to make it for the reading and hadn't shown up for rehearsal, I started to panic. We had three poems in which all of our voices were interwoven and they each had a poem to read with one other person, plus presenting their own original work. Jennifer shrugged and said, "How about if I invite another student to read Mikey's part and I will read Mai's?" She then explained that when Terence heard about the event, he had said to her, "Wouldn't it be cool to have a guest poet?" "Ok," I agreed. "Can he do the group poems?" "I will rehearse with him," she assured me. I didn't want to burden her with more work but she was dedicated to her students' success.

The day of the performance coincided with a full moon and perhaps that explains what happened next. I couldn't get internet on my computer so cell phone calls flew back and forth. Kimberly Nightingale, the executive director of Saint Paul Almanac, didn't know how many checks to prepare. Angela was too sick to come to school but was determined to make it to the reading. Tyler suddenly had an emergency visit to the hospital. Mikey was not answering his phone. Tonight was the college class that Chaunesty had signed up for; she had been emailing the professor but received no reply so she was on her way to the college to find out if she could be excused. I began to wonder if the show would happen at all.

There was nothing to do but surrender. Surely it would all work out, even if I had to do the entire show by myself. Panicking would not solve anything.

But at 6:45 pm, all the students except for Mikey had arrived. I put them to work distributing programs on the tables and arranging chairs while the soundman set up two mics. When he asked us to stand up, I suddenly realized that we were quite a range of heights, something I had not considered. The arriving audience seemed to be mostly students and school staff: the students had been promised extra credit in English. Out of the 200 friends from my email list that I had invited, three showed up. The artist who was to do an impromptu drawing of us while performing on stage had not appeared but the deaf signer who had not been available for the past three readings arrived ready to sign.

At 7:10, I was on stage. Mondays at the Black Dog had traditionally been slow but in order to draw in a crowd, Mondays were now game night. Besides the hiss of cappuccino machines, patrons on the other side of the café were loud and noisy. Kimberly made motions in the back to turn up the mics while I leaned forward to give my introduction. Static screeched between the mics, some students read softly, I couldn't tell if anyone in the audience could hear, although we soldiered bravely on.

"The moon is full," I announced, "and here we are in 2012. I am sorry for any difficulty in hearing us. We are doing our best to work with it." Halfway through, the light from the video production went out and the poem *I Give You Back* was recited without the use of the mics at all, because it was turned off when screeches filled the air.

But the show was a success. The audience loved it and showered us with enthusiastic applause. Jennifer's poem about being a teacher helped us to understand the world of these youth: did they have enough to eat, had they been awake at night with a cranky baby, exhausted from an after school job, what about their test scores and how can you infuse them with the love and joy of language when their current situations were tenuous and perhaps filled with violence and grief. The students spoke of what was on their minds, their desire to be heard. Their invented persona poems of teen pregnancy or being locked up may have been embellished by their imaginations, but they were based on people they knew. Their poems of love and sadness rang true. They were genuine and they were amazing.

You never know what to expect when you are working with young people. It keeps me on my toes, one of the reasons I love it. I feel proud when they are successful; it makes me want to try harder when my expectations are too high and they can't reach them. But best of all, students in the audience who had been ambiguous about attending the workshop left saying how inspired they were to take the next one. What will our next project be? I wonder. How can I get their voices out into the world?

Setting Intentions

Often I begin a writing class or workshop with setting our intentions. I ask writers to write for a few minutes what they hope to get out of the workshop, why they are taking the workshop and what they bring to the workshop. Usually we do not read this aloud. This is a way to begin with a short writing and to focus on why we are here. It is also a way to start the class by writing. I create a positive affirmation for myself and clarify my willingness to pay attention, to stay present, and to be of service. It serves as a reminder of what we hope to accomplish and to present ourselves as attentive and participatory. We can look back half-way through the workshop to see if we have held to our intention and at the end, to evaluate if we got what we wanted out of the workshop and if not, what questions are we left with? Perhaps we will be surprised along the way at how we met our intentions or at how something unexpected came up. If there is time, reading our intentions at the end of the class is a way to review what we learned.

My Intention for a class at Harriet Tubman Services for Victims of Domestic Violence:

> What I hope to get out of this class is an opportunity to explore more about patterns, my hopes and dreams, and to understand how I got from there to here. To acknowledge my strengths, to enjoy inspiration, to keep my feet on the path, to know the distance I have gone. What I hope is to be awake and receptive and to feel connected.

What I hope is to grow to become wiser, stronger and less held to my limitations. I hope to enjoy language and the joy of words.

My Intention for Restorative Justice class at Stillwater DOC:

My intention is to be present, to listen carefully, to guide the writer to find their own stories and to give guidance on craft. My intention is to be clear with instructions, to be fair and impartial, to give my presence, my talents, and my enthusiasm. To be encouraging and to help the writers shape their work into something meaningful.

My Intention for Story as Medicine: writing through grief

My intention is to be present, to listen with the ears of the heart, to create safety, intimacy and inspiration for the process to unfold. I hope for deeper awareness and deeper connection and to experience a transformative unfolding of whatever needs to come to the surface.

Another warm up exercise: How will I keep the fires burning?

I will keep the fires burning in my soul by keeping the writing moving, finding ways to renew my writing practice. I will keep the fire burning by meditation and prayer, literally lighting candles. Playing music I love. Being with family. Praying for peace. I will keep the fires burning by attending church and being uplifted by the choir. By giving gifts, by traveling the starry sky of hope. I will keep the fire of hope burning no matter how deep the darkness. I will find a way to celebrate the good and to honor the journey, how far I have come. I will find my way back to the deep gratitude and rest and peace. I will find ways to practice joy.

For writers:

The next exercise after setting intentions for a group of writers or those who are attending the workshop because they wish to improve their writing skills is to write on the topics of "My challenges, my strengths, and what I need help with." This will be the writing they will use to introduce themselves and it helps the instructor see what might be helpful to focus on or which craft lessons to present in the weeks to come.

Often when we begin a workshop, writers want to tell their stories, their history of writing practice. I choose to compost oral testimonies into writing, as much writing and less explaining as possible. I believe explaining will take energy away from the writing, that the emotional and revelatory impact will be diluted if we tell rather than write. I have also experienced in the Write Action writing support group a tendency to tell long stories about the previous week's trials and difficulties and turning the workshop into a support group rather than a writing group that is supportive. Be clear that this is a writing group and it can be therapeutic but it is not therapy. Use your material, what is on your mind, your hurt, disappointment, grief, bafflement, struggle, and anger to deepen the writing, is my theory.

This first exercise in articulating one's strengths and challenges will create a way to dialogue about the writers' expectation of themselves and the class. The writers in the class at Stillwater did not perceive their strengths as writers. This can be self-limiting and discouraging. It was evident that it was up to me to provide not only encouragement but to reflect back what was already working well.

To be required to articulate one's strengths is another way of honoring the writer who has a story to tell but may feel the critical judge telling him or her that he/she is not good enough. In order to move deeper into the intuitive imagination, to dive for the story that haunts us and will not let go or the story that is our transformative healing story, we need to silence the critic and pay attention to the innate storyteller.

WRITING SAMPLES

My challenge and strengths:

My challenge is to find the time to focus and to keep up with my blogs, to create fresh material while working on material already created. My strengths are a multitude of characters, many adventures, emotional depth and inspiration, My challenges is to not compare myself with other writers and get discouraged. My strength is persistence and not giving up. What I need help with is determining the starting place and which material is best to use and which is unnecessary.

My challenge and strengths:

My challenge is getting where I need to be. My challenge is feeling tired. My challenge is to keep the practice. My strengths are an open-heart, open mind, spiritually directed compassion. My strengths are to know myself and to take care of myself. My strengths are to keep moving forward and find inspiration, project ideas, network and community. My challenge is to continue submitting, to get back to the novel I started, and to focus on the new work as well as promoting old work. My strengths are the multi-faceted characters, multi-cultural settings, and the belief in a happy or at least satisfying ending.

What I need help with is humor and lightness.

Take a moment to write about your strengths as a writer. Are you good at description, do you have strong characters, do you create realistic dialogue? Do you have good plot ideas?

My strengths are

_____

_____

_____

_____

_____

_____

_____

Write about your challenges. Do you need better descriptions, well-rounded characters, pacing? Writing plot? Writing discipline? Motivation? Humor? Dialogue? Vocabulary?

My challenges are

_____

_____

_____

_____

_____

_____

_____

What do you need help with? What are your writing goals?

_____

_____

_____

_____

_____

_____

_____

_____

WARM UP EXERCISES:

Tell Your Story in One Minute

Count off in pairs. The prompt is a moment that changed your life. This exercise can begin with drawing a timeline for a few minutes. Draw a straight line down the page and draw branches for those moments that changed your life. I suggest dividing the timeline into decades and then draw branches off the time such as: first day of school, learning to read, learning to ride a bike, birth of sibling, learning to drive a car, first kiss, graduation, serious illness, first job, first true love, first heart break, marriage, divorce, children, death, travel, first time in real trouble, first spiritual crisis etc. I allow the group to work on this timeline for a few minutes, then explain that they can continue to work on it later.

Number 1 chooses one of these moments and has one and ½ minutes to tell the story to their partner Number 2.

Number 2 has a minute to tell their story to their partner Number 1.

We go around the circle and each person can tell their story in only three sentences.

Then I ask them to consider these questions and write about them for five minutes:

As the listener:

- What drew you into the other person's story?
- What detail was important?
- What questions did you have?
- Where did you connect and where didn't you?

As the teller:

- What was important to say?
- What didn't you get to say?
- How did the story begin?

- What felt important?
- How did it feel to be heard?

I also ask them to note where their attention was sparked and where they felt connected to the person telling the story.

I now tell the group that these moments that changed their lives are the places of their important stories, where the material is rich and juicy, and memory will be keen. These are transitional moments, threshold moments, where one's identity shifts from who you were before that moment to who you are afterwards. During the transition, you might feel you are in a luminal place where creativity flourishes. Your feelings might be complex. You might change your appearance, you might change your habits. You may break social taboos with permission or enter a new way of expressing yourself. You might go through the threshold as part of a community or become uniquely solo. Your insights, understanding and perspective may shift. You may remember sensory details vividly.

Circle one and write about it in a spontaneous writing and see where it leads. Use these moments as writing prompts. Writing about these pivotal moments may evoke memories, people, conversations, motivation, and lead to revelations or insights.

PROMPTS:

A moment that changed my life:

I can never forget

If I could change one thing

What I left behind and what I kept

POEM: Why I Write by Terry Tempest Williams

PROMPT: Why do you write?

Your Vein of Gold:

In her book *The Vein of Gold*, Julia Cameron talks about the vein of gold as the place where you will always give a good performance because it is where your passion and the problem you are trying to solve meet with your gift. She recommends an exercise of writing down movies you love, your favorite childhood book, three characters you loved, three characters you would like to play. She suggests that you name three topics you think about, and then ask if they have anything in common. Look at the lists: What problem are you trying to solve?

Here is my answer

My veil of gold is when I am honest on the page and transparent on the stage. When I can admit my pain, my anger, my confusion, and my joy in order to tell the story and connect with others. My vein of gold is story; I have hundreds and I love to tell them but I also love to provide the space and safety for others to tell theirs. By sharing my heart, I create intimacy and by using my words, I weave a web. Sometimes what I hear is astonishing. What fulfills me is to know I have created that space and then step back to let the work happen. The magic. The unfolding. My best work comes from knowing I have done whatever I can to build that bridge between us.

My favorite kids' books

The Little Engine that Could

The Secret Garden

Little Women

Jane Eyre

Old Yeller

My favorite movies

Like Water for Chocolate

Life is Beautiful

It's a Wonderful Life

The Wizard of Oz

The Secret of Roan Inish

(You can see a strong thread of magical surrealism in the movies I love.)

The problem I am working on is survival despite adversity, how to endure through ordeals, to keep my integrity and not give up, to keep my vision and ideals despite the harshness of the world. The problem is to remain true and to speak up as a woman, to express my passion without fear of how others will judge me.

Take Care of Yourself

Writing on a frequent basis will open your heart and uncover the stories you are compelled to tell. Memories will arise, uncomfortable feelings will stir, grief and regrets, guilt or disappointment, unresolved hurt or unhealed wounds, as well as insights, new perspectives and hidden meanings. As the writing facilitator, I write with the group and share my writing. What I learned as a writing instructor/facilitator is that when I write, there are two paths. One will take me deeper and deeper into the story: what happened to me and what I feel about it. There is no end to that branch of the story. I can tell it over and over, because the emotional pull is powerful. Or I can choose another branch: what it means, what patterns I see, where it leads me, what has been the lesson, and how I can change or be transformed because of it. And as the leader responsible for the circle, I deliberately choose that branch. That is what I write about and share. When I led workshops under the funding of the grant, writing with battered women and homeless youth and heart patients and care-givers, I was writing weekly or twice weekly and choosing that path over and over again. What does it mean to me, what did I learn, where do I find inner courage and strength, what do I still have, what are my blessings? And I began to heal, not only enough to keep going, not only enough to be engaged with laughter and friendship and love and curiosity and pleasure, but real joy. An inner knowing that I am where I am meant to be, that I am living my dreams, that I am connected to others in deep ways and that I love my life. I am blessed. I am grateful.

Although I share my writing with the group, I am mindful not to burden the group with taking care of me. I share my struggles, failures, and griefs; I am vulnerable on the page. But I also edit as I read aloud if the material I have written seems inappropriate or will necessitate the group taking care of me. A delicate balance must be maintained between a group resonance of taking care of each other and staying objective enough to oversee the entire group dynamic. There is an inherent imbalance of power in the position of leadership. I am especially aware of this when teaching in the prison. I want to be personal without losing my professionalism. It is not their job to comfort or console me although it is necessary to feel connected and to be my authentic self and of course, to share the struggles and triumphs of being a writer.

It is essential for you as the writing facilitator to take care of yourself. When I taught the class at Stillwater prison for the purpose of holding a reading during Victim Awareness Week, I knew I would have to find ways to nurture my own creative rejuvenation. I knew the material we would be working with would be very emotional, and although I knew I would remain calm, receptive, and present during our workshop time together, there could be a backwash afterwards. I choose to leave town twice during this time. Once was to attend a workshop presented by David Whyte at the Sophia Institute in Charleston, South Carolina. I flew into Charleston two days prior to the workshop so I would have an entire day to explore the town. The weather was balmy and the townspeople warmly hospitable. I left the workshop filled with light and this gave me a cushion to return to the hard work of the prison workshop.

The second time I taught at a women's retreat called Celebrate Yourself. I knew some of the women who would be attending, and my previous experience of spending a weekend in the woods with a group of women was that we laughed and joked and shared stories and encouraged and uplifted each other in a gentle conviviality. And so it was.

Ways to take care of ourselves:

- walk or do yoga or dance, hang out in nature, feel the sun on your face or sit by a body of water, massage, cuddle, have sex, eat healthy foods. Any activity that occupies your immediate attention and gives you a break from over-thinking can help soothe and restore.

- talk with a trusted friend or counselor, read uplifting messages, express love for family and friends, feel heard, discuss other topics, laughter

- create and repeat positive affirmations, participate in a spiritual community, sing, chant or listen to music, meditation and prayer: quiet the mind down

- make art or visit a museum, being inspired by others' work will raise your vibration

Other possibilities:

- write a letter to someone you admire, expressing your admiration and gratitude, write letter to someone in your writing world (a writing partner, an imaginary agent or editor, a writer you admire) explaining what you are working on and your intended goals, write a letter to a reader, explaining why you need to write your story

- Keep a blessing journal:

Every day write down three blessings. Note any blessings such as a friend called, a new book to read, a good meal, a cleaned kitchen, a gorgeous sunset, an inspiring poem, help with a project, a favorite song, a great parking spot, the bus on time, a smile from a stranger

- If the material is too hard to write, write in third person and/or turn it into fiction

You can go back and rewrite in first person. Sometimes we need to the distance of third person to get our emotions on the page. Turning it fiction will give us permission to explore other points of view and perspectives.

- Write your story with a successful outcome or amazing synchronicities or with the ending you dream of.

- Give yourself a break from the dissection of your self to the vision of what you can be. I once threw a "Come as you want to be" party. I arrived dressed up for my trip to accept the Nobel Prize. Even though it was a fantasy, it gave me momentum to keep going at a time when I felt discouraged. The Nobel Prize may be out of reach but I published two books of poetry and have performed for hundreds of audience members, have won four grants and have been able to teach in prisons and non-profits, schools and healing centers. Besides my work appearing in literary journals and anthologies, I had an article published in *Poets & Writers magazine*. The momentum to believe in myself pushed me through that critical voice, that one we all have in our heads, that says I am not good enough, made the wrong choices, or can't compete.

It is important to create positive affirmations and listen to them. I have several taped onto my computer: "You're transforming yourself into someone who is certain to succeed" is from a fortune cookie and "I reach my destiny by achieving prosperity and leadership with grace and ease." I read them daily.

I also keep this quote handy:

Have faith in tomorrow; enjoy today as you learn that all existence rests in a circle of love. Strive for an understanding heart filled with sympathy and hopefulness toward others. Dare to dream, dare to think, and dare to act as power flows from your mind. Expect new revelations of truth as your thoughts build and create wherever you are and whatever you desire. Understand that you are not the first to suffer, love, or prosper, and that life, despite changes is always a measure of the legacy our ancestors left. Accept the lessons and the experiences of the past, taking the best from all that has occurred, and press boldly into the future, moving closer and closer to your goal. Understand connections; we are all mutually dependent, and the circle of life goes ever onward.

- Take a break and write something else: poetry, short story, flash fiction

Come as you want to be as you rewrite your work: wiser, stronger, happier, beloved, and doing what you love to do. Keep your vision of your published book in your hand, your audience enthralled. Imagine the questions your interviewer will ask. Know that you have a story to tell that will open hearts and minds.

WRITING EXERCISES

- How to use Have a _____ Day by by Lou Lipsitz

Write a list: favorite foods, a movie, the name of a movie star, the name of a song, an historical moment in your lifetime, a weather condition

Read the poem Have a _____ Day.

Write your own poem using your list

Write on slips of colored paper: your favorite food, the name of a song, a movie star, a historical moment in your lifetime, a weather condition. Use a particular color for each category. Exchange slips or make a pile in the middle and each writer chooses slips, making sure he has one color from each category. Use them to write your own Have a _____ Day poem.

1. Write a piece of advice, a cliché, or a superstition on a slip of paper, pass it to your neighbor. That is the prompt.

2. Fortune Cookie: Write something you might find in a fortune cookies: pass it to your neighbor. That is the prompt.

3. Write a lie on a piece of paper such as I grow ants in my bathtub. My family is from Mars. Make a pile and each writer chooses one. Use it as your prompt.

4. Write down a secret. Without disclosing the secret, write something that reveals it through sensual imagery such as sound, scent, taste, touch, sight. Use the sensory experiences and body language show how you felt. Let everyone guess the secret.

Why I Write: The Wounded and Enduring

(previously published in *Poets & Writers Magazine* July/August 2014)

For ten weeks at a time on a week-day evening, I am locked into a room with seven-fifteen men at Stillwater prison in Bayport, Minnesota for a writing class. Stillwater is a correctional facility for level 4 offenders. Their sentences range from twenty-thirty years to life. I don't ask what crimes they have committed; I don't want that to stand between us but often, in a piece they have written or during a conversation, they give clues. One man has let me know his "bid" is life plus twenty-five, another has double life sentences, and one tells me he has survived twenty-one years so far and talks about "when he gets out."

With the men at Stillwater, I tread carefully a tightrope between being honest and holding back. In our orientation, we were coached never to reveal anything personal. It could be used to target us in some way or, at least, asked for favors. If anyone ever tries to contact us outside of class, we have to report it immediately; it is simply not allowed.

Despite the bars and grey walls, the clanging of steel doors, the lingering smell of past meals, the guard in the bubble room, the "screecher" to pull in an emergency, once we are locked in, there are no distractions. It is quiet but for occasional noise in the hallway as inmates transfer to their cells. We are focused. I am always amazed at the variety of voices and responses to a writing exercise. I know we each have a story to tell, but the stories I hear in this setting are powerful and painful. There are times when I have to walk gingerly over the boundaries of writing instructor to respond as a human being, as a spiritual human being, to writings about suicide, abandonment from family, guilt and regret over the past that cannot be changed, what it means to grow up in an institution where one is not able to make choices except whether or not to break a rule and get thrown into seg (segregation). I listen to stories about what it means to lose years of one's life.

A precious freedom these writers have lost is the ability to interact though their work with the outside world. They are not allowed Internet access yet most of them want publication, a desire I know well. Some have been writing for years and are working on long works: science fiction, fantasy, crime drama, memoir. When we discuss publishing, I feel frustrated and falsely optimistic. I recommend resources but I can't give them access to those I myself use. I can't add my own poetry collection to the prison library, since it is a collection of love poems and far too personal. The topic of research comes up frequently. How to describe the streets of a town one may never see again without the use of something as elemental as a map?

I ask myself: why do we do it? Why do *I* do it? The facile answer is that I believe in the Golden Rule, that what I give away will come back to me. I believe that institutions are inhumane ways to deal with those who aren't part of our consumer oriented culture. I do it to bring light into dark places, to contribute to making peace in a world where violence is one of the reasons they are locked up, where violence can erupt at any moment, where violence may have become a way of expressing the anger and frustration they feel.

But I also do it because of writing. The writer in me is awed by the resiliency of the human spirit, by the tears one man shed in a class held at Moose Lake when we read Joy Harjo's poem *I Give You Back*, by the thoughtful, impassioned response to Adrienne Rich's poem XIII *(Dedications)*. One of the more experienced writers said that the bars melt away he is writing. My bars melt away, too. The bars that keep me inside my head instead of opening up; the bars of judgment; the bars that make me feel alone, abandoned, different; the bars born of the broken heartedness of life.

I am not locked up, of course, I can change my mind or my perspective. Writing helps me do that. I have suffered losses of a partner and a son to suicide, plunging me into a dark night that seemed unbearable. Every day I had to convince myself to go on. When I was young I was kidnapped at gun point and raped. I sent that man to prison for more than 150 years because he had escaped from a federal penitentiary and had a weapon. In the course of the 4 hours he held me hostage, he had threatened to shoot me and then himself. I talked him down by asking him to tell me his story, a story of a mild-mannered drug addict sent to prison for forging a check and being battered and beaten, humiliated and harmed so that he wanted to take it out on someone else.

I write in prison because I am writing together with people who made bad choices, often under the influence, or who have mental illnesses, or who were brought up in a street culture where it seemed necessary to kill or be killed. And haven't I often made bad choices, haven't I felt on the edge of madness and break down and inability to function? I can't say I have ever had enough rage to kill someone but I know what it is like to make one fatal decision that entraps you into a situation that is wrong and impossible to change without sacrificing pride or soul.

The writing we do together is deep and honest and sharp and imaginative and sweet and poignant. I write with the wounded and I write with the enduring. One man writes that his hidden blessing was that his parents beat him to show they care. Another writes about how he watched his mother take a bullet after a car full of men called out a racial epitaph, then sped away. One man writes about learning of his father's death when he was nine years old. The assignment was to write about a moment that changed your life. After he read it, his voice quavering, he said, "If I had known you were going to ask us to read our homework, I never would have written this." One of our most prolific, thoughtful, talented writers writes about his family discovering a

89

four year old boy abandoned on the street on Christmas day and calling social services to pick him up, how it changed his view of the world, how the world no longer seemed safe. One writes about his cousin's suicide in the tier above his. So as the teacher, I listen, I acknowledge, I respond with my heart, then I say, "Let's take a look at how you wrote that dialogue. Let's discuss your use of adjectives. Your ending. Your characters." I am not a therapist. I am a writer.

Here is a quote from Jennifer in an article she wrote called *Dear World: Postcards From A Prison Teacher:* "I once heard a woman say that when you become a prisoner in our culture, you're defined by your worst moment for the rest of your life. Indeed, writing reminds us that we have many moments by which to define ourselves fully. Art offers openings; to provide access to it is humane, also logical."

I also write with those who thirst for self-awareness and change, who have been transformed from understanding the choices they made, who are still positive and optimistic and tender and count their blessings and want to soar above their circumstances by the written word, the way it gives us wings and ignites our minds. By a more experienced writer saying to the beginner writers, "We want to welcome you. Don't feel intimidated because we have been writing a longer time and it might seem like we're better writers." Yes, I remind them, we all started somewhere. We laugh and joke and talk about TV shows, too. And here I must mention the tremendous support we have received from the DOC, the education directors rearranging schedules to accommodate us, the warden attending readings, the offer to buy books and certificates handed out at the end of a completed class.

One of the writing exercises I gave in my second class was based on an article about Wabi-Sabi, the art of imperfection, by Briana Crusan. She wrote, "You buy a vase and it breaks, you then glue the pieces back together but you can still see the lines between the pieces. This makes the vase more beautiful because now it has a story, character, and meaning." Someone in my class responds: "Writing has glued my shattered life back together into a functional piece again. It has imbued my life with meaning and purpose. Miraculously, this is happening in prison."

I, too, know what it is to have my life shattered and glued back together by writing. And as well, my life came together by showing up in places where the darkness lingers and can catch hold, by passing along what I know, by deep listening and paying attention, and by telling the story of how I survived and healed. I can not imagine what it would be like to have those doors clang shut, my freedom gone, freedom to move and to plan my own day. I can not imagine what it is like to be scrutinized or have my cell shaken down for contraband or to have to put up a façade of toughness. I own my body as well as my thoughts. I am grateful every day for the life I have created but especially when I walk out the doors of Stillwater. We do not leave them behind us when we walk away; this is something else we have learned. They stay in our hearts and minds. We, too, wish they had made different choices. We, too, feel broken hearted at their existence behind razor wire and walls. But we come together as human beings and for a few hours, that is all we are.

WRITING EXERCISE: with men at Stillwater-MCF: level 4 offenders

POEM: Crying Poem by Jimmy Santiago Baca

PROMPT: What messages did you receive when you were growing up about becoming a man?

What do you believe about being a man now?

CLASS DISCUSSION: As each writer read his piece, I was intrigued by how differently each responded to the prompt. One wrote about entering incarceration as a teen and how the environment keeps him in a state of false adolescence. Another wrote about seeing his father cry for the first time and how shocking it was. One wrote about being a father and yet unable to raise his child and take responsibility. One wrote about being the tough guy, not allowing himself to cry. One wrote about crying secretly, only if alone.

It struck me that growing up in any institutional setting whether it be a boarding school, monastery, prison, or armed services is a type of prolonged adolescence because you do not have the autonomy to make decisions and choices except to break rules and be punished. You do not have the opportunity to make mistakes that lead to insight or self-knowledge or natural consequences. The consequences are sometimes arbitrary and dependent on those in authority.

In the workshop I asked: How do you mature in an institutional setting? How do you make choices that change your days into destiny rather than being a victim of your previous choices, your personality, your powerlessness? How do you move forward to becoming a man you can admire and look up to when you have deep remorse and regrets? Can you access those tears to write onto the page? Write about what makes you cry.

PROMPT SUGGESTIONS FOR INCARCERATED WRITERS

ICEBREAKERS:

Set intentions for class: Why are you here, what do you hope to get out of the class, what do you bring to the class?

I knew I was in trouble when….

The first time

a moment that changed my life

what I lost and what I was able to keep

Hand out a card with these on it:

PICK A PROMPT TO START YOUR STORY: HE, SHE OR I

In his pocket, he had…

When she arrived to………………, she said …

It was twilight but the lights weren't on yet.

He smelled danger as soon as he…

"Put that down!" she shouted.

For the sake of…

It was out of his hands, he …

Stop!

I imagine you had to……

POEM: Kindness by Naomi Shihab Nye

PROMPT: what I left behind

PROMPT: It was a day like any other: start with something ordinary, describe the setting and yourself doing an ordinary activity, then something extraordinary, unexpected happens

POEM: Oranges by Gary Soto

PROMPT: the story I am compelled to tell

POEM: Consider the Hands that Write This Letter by Aracelis Girmay

PROMPT: the two parts of me: right/ left, light/ dark, aware/ unaware, strong/ weak etc

POEM: BORROWER by Una Nichols Hynum

PROMPTS: what am I doing here

Where did I come from, what do I want?

POEM: Alabanza by Martin Espada

PROMPT: Write an ode, a poem of praise to something that is hard to praise. Look for the hidden blessings

POEM: Passover by Lynn Ungar

PROMPT: leave room for the mystery

POEM: Courage by Anne Sexton

PROMPTS: What gives me courage

How do I hold onto my inner truth?

What sustains me?

POEM: I Give You Back by Joy Harjo

PROMPT: what do you release: choose an abstract quality: fear, doubt, loneliness, sorrow, despair, envy, greed, anger etc

POEM: The Journey by Mary Oliver

PROMPT: my own inner voice

POEM: Hook by James Baldwin

PROMPTS: the gift he/ she gave me

an unexpected kindness

POEM: Longing Inspired by the Law of Gravity by Fadwa Touqan

PROMPT: there is nothing like…..

POEM: Otherwise by Wislawa Symborsky

PROMPT: if I could change one thing

PROMPTS:

A time I was terrified

What I yearn for

Something of my own

Negotiate or submit

Lucky or unlucky

My miracle

I'll never forget

The turning point

It's never too late

I can't live without

Only a glance

Oddly enough

Create a perfect world: describe what it would look like, smells, tastes, light, sounds

If anyone strikes my heart, it does not break, but it bursts, and the flame coming out of it becomes a torch on my path. —Hazrat Inayat Khan

There's a lovely Hasidic story of a rabbi who always told his people that if they studied the Torah, it would put scriptures on their hearts. One of them asked, "Why on our hearts, and not in them?" The rabbi answered, "Only God can put scripture inside. But reading sacred text can put it on your hearts, and then when your hearts break, the holy words will fall inside."

—Anne Lamott in *Plan B: Further Thoughts on Faith*

PROMPTS: What is written on your heart?

What is the flame that lights your path?

HOMEWORK IDEAS:

a letter to my younger self/ a young man

a letter from the future self to my present self

what I say to my heart, how my heart responds

message in a bottle

what the oracle told me

I come from / I am

use songs, fashions, car models, neighborhood, food, historical moments or figures to describe who you are

Example: I come from chicken soup with the feet left in the pot

back in my day

my grandmother /mother/ grandfather/ father told me:

POEM: Some Advice to those who will serve time in prison by Nazim Hikmet

PROMPTS: What advice would you give to others?

I wish they had told me

if I had done things differently

a time someone lied to me

POEM: What is broken is what God blesses by Jimmy Santiago Baca

PROMPT: finding the blessing

or the best mistake I ever made

POEM: Silences by Diane Ackerman

PROMPT: there are many forms of: choose an abstract quality: justice, kindness, boredom, loneliness, knowledge, sadness, dreams, gratitude and interweave concrete specific details with abstract universal qualities

Hands say / eyes say/ feet say/ bones say

POEM: The Journey by David Whyte

PROMPT: what new thing is written in the ashes of your life

POEM: Dedications by Adrienne Rich

PROMPT: what are you dedicated to

Anne Lamott: essay *Forgiveness* from *Traveling Mercies: Some Thoughts on Faith*

write about forgiveness: forgiveness lite: something or someone that is easy to forgive

forgiveness: what would forgiveness look like

move on to someone it is hard to forgive: if this is hard, try changing to third person

POEM: Florida Room by Richard Blanco

PROMPT: where I feel safe

a memory of a place from childhood

POEM: The Journey by Mary Oliver

PROMPT: mend my life

POEM: Sweet Darkness by David Whyte

PROMPT: what brings you alive

from Gabrielle Roth:

In many shamanic societies, if you came to a medicine person complaining of being disheartened, dispirited or depressed, they would ask you one of four questions. When did you stop dancing? When did you stop singing? When did you stop being enchanted by stories? When did you stop finding comfort in the sweet territory of silence?

Questions to Deepen Your Writing Practice

How can you continue to write?

_____

_____

_____

_____

_____

_____

What are you afraid to write about?

_____

_____

_____

_____

_____

_____

What are you compelled to write about?

_____

_____

_____

_____

_____

_____

What story do you need to tell?

_____

_____

_____

_____

_____

What do you want people to know about you?

_____

_____

_____

_____

_____

How can you view your actions from a different point of view?

_____

_____

_____

_____

_____

Unchained Voices

When I think of what it means to leave a legacy, I think about teaching creative writing in prison. As a writer, my dream is to leave a legacy of my own words, my published works. But by teaching in prison, my desire to make the world a better place complements my desire to pass on my passion for language and story; my desire to be of service dances with my desire to be visible, heard, understood and respected. My wisdom gained from many life experiences, from scraping together meals for 100 homeless adults in Portland to feeding soup to run-aways in the streets of Seattle, from hitch-hiking across Mexico and begging for meals to sitting guard duty at my son's public school in Israel during the Intifada, is melded to my gift.

I had taught many kinds of writing classes by the time I came to Stillwater Department of Corrections: at women's retreats with women blocked by the ways they had been silenced, with youth in crisis who feel unsafe and unwanted, at bookstores where people wandered in, at healing centers delving into what needs to be released, at Unity church where we cared for our souls and at Pathways, caring for ourselves so we could care for others. Writing is a beautiful way to examine one's own heart and reading your words aloud is a way to connect. Writing is disturbing, although it also creates the calming chemicals in the brain of serotonin and dopamine; it shakes things awake that are dormant and reveals what is deepest within.

Incarcerated writers want to be heard and yet have severe limitations to getting an audience. They have limited access to computers and little or no internet access, especially challenging in a literary world where submittable is the preferred means of submissions, and often with a fee. They cannot attend AWP conferences, writers' festivals, or take workshops at literary centers or colleges, cannot meet agents, or learn how to develop a platform. They do not have the means to self-publication. They usually can't gather with other writers to discuss craft or attend readings. The writing life is often a lonely, solitary path and I appreciate every chance I get to chat with other writers, to learn from their triumphs and challenges, to get feedback on my projects and to network and schmooze for the fun of being with my tribe: people who understand me. Grasping a new way to approach a topic from a craft talk interwoven into the hours spent at the desk with pencil and paper or at the computer has often saved me from giving up.

This is the reason I was inspired to write *Heart on the Page*. The writer behind bars and razor wire relies on us to bring the workshop to *him or her*. The writers with an urgency to tell their stories and can't figure out where to start or where to find an audience, the writers who can't stroll down to the café, call a friend, or spend time in nature or at a residency or retreat, they are my motivations for writing this book.

In the late '80s, when I lived communally, I visited a prisoner at Oregon State Penitentiary and I corresponded with pen-pals from several state prisons. I am familiar with isolation and separation and loneliness that they expressed in their letters, the heartbreak of powerlessness and loss of identity.

I believe that we are not our circumstances, that we are souls having a human experience which include mistakes and failures. I believe that we each must save ourselves by inner change and that we can soar free if we don't let the system, our self-doubt and our bad choices define who we are meant to become.

I believe in transformation and growth. This can happen in prison.

Stillwater is a level 4 facility; the men receive terms of 20 years to life. I soon learned that the participants in my first class were invited based on their involvement in personal growth, attending Building Character classes, the

Restorative Justice program and/or college classes. What they didn't know and I didn't realize, was that their proposal to create a writers' collective and MPWW's proposal to teach dovetailed at the same time. It wasn't until the last day of class that I found out that these goals had suddenly synchronized. It certainly felt like fate.

From the beginning, I was astonished at the high level of writing skills of the experienced writers and how quickly beginners improved. I was blown away by the depth of the work written during class, our concentrated focus in the classroom, and the quality of the homework assignments they turned in. I had to come up with a variety of ideas and writing exercises to stretch the experienced writers and give the beginners confidence. We generated material in class and concluded with a chapbook published by Red Bird Chapbooks and video-taped a class reading. When asked if they would like to broadcast the reading over the facility's public access channel, they said no, the writing was too personal. This was to change over time and in 2014, the reading was the intention and goal of the Restorative Justice class.

I was invited by the Stillwater Writers' Collective to teach a class with the purpose of holding an in-house reading during National Victim Awareness week. They wanted to express their remorse for Victim Services and Restorative Justice programs to hear and to demonstrate the benefits of writing for Victim Services —the mission of Minnesota correctional facilities is, after all, to rehabilitate. Although we didn't yet have documented proof, studies show writing not only improves thinking and reasoning skills but leads to empathy and positive engagement with others. My article had just been published in *Poets & Writers Magazine* and the organizer of the SWC told me it gave me credibility to lead this class on top of their personal experience of my teaching style. In the article, I wrote about my struggle to heal after being a victim of violence. I wrote about the profound impact that teaching in prison had on me as a writer as well as a human being.

I was honored to teach this course. I also knew that we could not stay focused on emotions of regret. We particularly needed to clarify that these men had changed and were not capable of committing these crimes ever again, that they not only felt remorse but were making different choices; they were in counseling for anger management and self-awareness; they were dedicated to self-improvement. Those invited to this class had spent years in personal development classes, working with the Restorative Justice Program, earning degrees. Most were serious writers—writing poetry, short stories, plays, essays and memoir. I later learned that some inmates were afraid to take the class if they had any appeals or were about to come before the parole board as it seemed an admission of guilt. But admitting guilt was not a problem for these writers. They were burdened by relentless guilt.

I was surprised by their candor and willingness to share stories of painful childhood abuse and identification with their victim. I was struck by their sense of dying to a previous identity and the struggle to be reborn as a man rather than a perpetrator. They wrote about hitting bottom and the determination to change. They wrote about suicide attempts and second chances. They wrote about family members that visit and family members who have abandoned them. One wrote in the persona of the victim's daughter who had attended his trial and handed him a cross, saying, "Pass it on to whoever you meet who needs forgiveness more than you do." They wrote from the viewpoint of the victim and the viewpoint of a house left empty after someone has died. They wrote about the letters their victim's family sent them and what it must have felt like to identify a son's body. A social worker from Restorative Justice wrote with us and her writing was heartfelt and honest. She wrote about the impact of her infidelity on her family. The men were very moved by her willingness to share.

While visiting a friend in Chicago, I had the opportunity to see a documentary about an artist on the East Coast who had been invited to facilitate an art project to bring together inmates and the local Restorative Justice group. The inmates wanted to paint a mural as a gift to the group. The artist helped them design a mural which she felt was a vivid cry of reaching out; the victims or survivors would have none of it. The victims said the mural's design showed the inmates' perspectives and was not reflective of their experience. A meeting was arranged to discuss the mural and the victims were angry, accusatory and brutally honest. They said things such as *My life has been ruined, my family is devastated.* "How dare you ask me for forgiveness? I don't have to forgive you," one said with contempt and tears. The artist was surprised and especially daunted at finding herself between these two groups with no training in mediation. She listened and facilitated, allowing them to come to their own solution. A compromise was reached. Two murals were designed to be hung on the walls of two buildings one block apart, so that you could view both from the corner, a dialogue but not a direct connection.

The canvases of the murals were divided into sections, almost like a giant paint-by-number and the victim/survivors group came inside the facility to help paint the canvases. It was while painting together that the process of healing began. Victims were able to express their hurt and how hard it had been to keep going and inmates shared stories of childhood abuse and the punitive results of their crimes. In this real dialogue, the participants started to see each other as human beings dealing with grief, tragedy, trauma, and their aftermath.

I began our writing process by asking the participants to write about a time they had been afraid or intimidated or lost. I wanted them to tap into their own painful memories as a stepping stone to writing about their victims with empathy. I also thought that it was important to see a link between their wounds, often unhealed abuse and unacknowledged grief, and the crimes they had committed. Then I asked them to write about how their crimes had impacted their families. This brought it close to the bone. Writers wrote about loss of family connections, of aunts coming to visit and leaving in sorrow, dads who write only occasionally, grandfathers who were never informed of what happened to their favorite grandson, a letter to a mom who used to beat her son.

I am always aware that writing like this is therapeutic but I am not a therapist. I believe in the healing power of writing itself, that what needs to surface will surface and that writing is like a miner's pickaxe to mine what is ready to be excavated. But I was surprised at how the men were able to write about the past without describing the sequence of events, to be able to say "I am a murderer" without defensiveness. I also found out that many of them knew their victims and some had been friends and fellow trouble-makers long before the climax of events that led to their incarceration. I can not help but think that writing the truth was cathartic for them. I know one man impressed his counselor to the point that she changed his counseling appointments so he could attend our class.

The class then focused on the impact on their victim's families. I started with a list of PTSD symptoms. This hit them hard. These symptoms are real and life altering, they can go on for years, and may require therapy or counseling to heal. We used Gregory Orr's poem *Gathering the Bones Together* as a prompt jump-start. It is a poem about a boy accidently shooting his brother, a hard poem to teach in a prison setting. This is the second section:

A father and his four sons

run down a slope toward

a deer they just killed.

The father and two sons carry

rifles. They laugh, jostle,

and chatter together.

A gun goes off

and the youngest brother

falls to the ground.

A boy with a rifle

stands beside him,

screaming.

and in the 7th section he writes:

I was twelve when I killed him;
I felt my own bones wrench from my body.

The writing opened at this point. In many ways, it is almost impossible to imagine how difficult it must be to be a survivor of your own bad choice. Imagination to place ourselves in the other person's shoes also necessitates respect for their experience. We discussed the question of do we have the right to write about someone else's experience? I assured them that if done with respect and care, it is a way to understand the depth of that experience and we should not shy away from allowing it to impact us.

The writing moved from raw to powerful. The next session focused on the impact their crimes had on their victims. One wrote about living out the life his victim will never have: the way he feels bound for eternity by the choice he made. One wrote about the bullet next to his victim's heart and how it could kill him at any time; he never stops thinking about it.

Most of the writing was done in between classes as homework. In class we shared our work and critiqued it with these simple questions:

- What struck you? What stood out and what resonated?
- What was unclear or unnecessary?
- What did you need more of?
- Was there a twist or surprise?
- Was there a risk in emotion or content?

I interwove listening and critiquing with other kinds of writing exercises, to alleviate the heaviness and painfulness of the writing. We usually finished class with a writing exercise. Some writing prompts were:

- Ready or not
- It's never too late
- What gives me courage
- The gift she/he gave me

- I can't live without
- Advice from the oracle
- Imagine you are published. What interview question would you like to be asked?
- Write down a lie. Pass it to the next person as a prompt
- Praying for….
- Only a glance
- Oddly enough
- Pass out slips of paper with nouns: specific place, specific name of a person and specific adjectives: (individuals might include famous actors, writers or sports figures such as Michael Jackson, Anderson Cooper, Julia Roberts, Tim O'Brien, Maeve Binchy, Cheryl Strayed, or made up names: Roy Smith, Jose Portalles, Lulu James: they do not have to know who the character is. The places are actual locations and might include: Whole Foods, Walmart, the movie theater, the corner of Snelling and University, Como Park, etc. Each writer chooses one of each, a character, a place and an adjective to include in their writing

1. Describe the quality of light: day/night, sunny/stormy/gloomy, time of year, natural/ artificial light to set the mood

2. You encounter the person you picked. You need to make a decision. Write for five minutes.

3. Pass your person to the next writer. This new character offers his or her opinion to the character you just wrote about. Write for five more minutes

4. Read what you wrote. Sure to induce laughter.

- Begin with a setting. In 4 sentences describe the setting. You need to make a choice. Don't tell us which choice you made, just show inner conflict

I brought a handout culled from a website called perfectapology.com that defined the difference between regret and remorse as a basis for discussion: "Regret is a rational, intelligent and on occasion emotional reaction to some unexpected, unintended and often costly consequence of some event or action. Remorse, on the other hand, takes on a bitter, deeper form that elicits much stronger personal and emotional reactions to personal guilt, societal shame, humiliation, resentment and often anger." I explained the word *metanoia*: a transformative change of heart. "This is what you need to write about," I told them. "You can't change the past and you can't expect to be forgiven by the person or family you hurt. But you can show how you have achieved *metanoia*. You can receive forgiveness, but maybe not from your victim or victim's family. I believe forgiveness is available to all of us as an on-going process."

This led us to our final writing: our healing stories. I read an excerpt from Matthew Sanford's memoir *Waking*. He became a paraplegic resulting from a car accident and learned to use yoga to send energy through his body. He now runs a non-profit, teaches yoga to others who are not disabled as well as the disabled, and makes presentations about healing through yoga. He wrote in his book *Waking: A Memoir of Trauma and Transcendence* (Rodale, 2006)

Two important descriptive terms appear throughout my story: *silence* and *healing stories.* Silence is the word I use to describe the empty presence we experience within our experience—between our thoughts, between each other, between ourselves and the world. We feel the silence when we daydream, when we appreciate the beauty of a sunset, or when the love of our life truly walks away. It is an inward sense, often experienced as a longing or an ache. It is a feeling of emptiness and fullness at the same time. It does require, however, that I seek more profoundly within my own experience and do so with an open mind. It means that I must reach intuitively into what may feel like darkness.

A healing story is my term for the stories we have come to believe that shape how we think about the world, ourselves, and our place in it. … Healing stories guide us through good and bad times; they can be both constructive and destructive, and are often in need of change.

Our healing stories were eloquent reminders that each man had chosen to work on himself, that each carried the burden of remorse while also moving forward into growth, change and transformation. The social worker who participated in our class reminded them of all that they had accomplished when waves of self-incrimination swept through the classroom. We talked about mentoring younger men or helping those adjusting to life inside or just lending a hand and being a good person. We titled the reading "Unchained Voices."

"Unchained Voices" proved to be profoundly moving, beyond anything I expected. Our audience of about seventy-five included MPWW instructors, staff from administration, Restorative Justice, and Victim Services, the warden, the commissioner and his assistant, as well as members of a community non-profit organization. Each incarcerated writer from the class was able to invite two inmates. SWC printed up gorgeous hand-lettered programs and a banner.

When I arrived, the men asked me if I was nervous. I would only introduce the reading and read one poem, but I could tell *they* were extremely nervous. They insisted I read something, I was part of the team, so I would share a piece I had written in class called "My Voice" to kick off the final section of our inner transformations.

Our program began with a funny but poignant story of being bullied by a girl in elementary school.

Despite weeks of revisions and a rehearsal, the fourth reader broke down at the podium. I saw the box of Kleenex handed up and down as each story unfolded, and by the time we reached the section of the impact of their crimes on their families, much of the audience was in tears as well. During intermission, people came up to shake hands and wipe away tears. The final section "Man in the Mirror" was powerful and cathartic.

One of our instructors said it was the most extraordinary event he had ever been to. I think he expressed what many of us felt. We were seeing these men, most in prison for murder, as human beings. Their remorse can never be put to rest, the desire for forgiveness and absolution and redemption is intense and constant, but they have worked *hard* to change.

It is essential after an emotional and cathartic reading such as this to hold a debriefing class. Check in with each writer as to how he is doing, how he experienced the reading and what has changed internally. Praise their courage and their vulnerability and the impact of that on others. A few writing exercises can help to diffuse any lingering tension or emotional overload but allow plenty of time for the writers to express whatever is on their minds.

POEM: Santiago by David Whyte

PROMPT: what beckons, what leads you on

POEM: The Journey by David Whyte

PROMPT: What new thing is written in the ashes of your life?

Read the essay *Confessions* from *Consolations* by David Whyte and ask for comments. Or sit silently for a moment and take it in.

Stillwater's education director Pat Pawlack, who had done so much to make the class and the reading happen, including sending personal invitations, was deeply moved. When she visited our debriefing meeting, said she was surprised at how vulnerable and candid the writers had been, the risks they took.

One writer said that he was surprised by his tears. He had read his pieces over and over, revising again and again, but in reading them aloud to an audience, he actually *heard* his own words. One commented on how the class helped him to stop judging others by the outward façade and be more compassionate. Another said he thought others would see him as weak but he was surprised that they wanted to hug him. And later, in our monthly forum, one writer mentioned that instead of acting in anger after an incident, he had gone back to his cell to write. The effects rippled through the cellblocks and through administration.

The power of writing was demonstrated in that reading. To me, this is what writing is all about. To change, to be changed, to have a voice, to be heard, to be visible, to reach out to someone's heart and touch it in ways that are irrevocable. People were calling it a once in a lifetime experience. This was beyond the inmate who told us that now he and his family recite poems to each other over the phone after taking one of our classes. This experience altered our lives forever.

Spiritual Memoir

Despite all the things that happened in my life, I never lost my faith—until I lost my son. One of the most painful aspects of his death was how my anger shook my faith to the core. I knew, somehow, that I had the spiritual resources from my years of spiritual practice: prayer, meditation, devotion. But I could not access them. It would take months and years to retrieve my belief in a Higher Power for the Good. It would take sharing my poetry in cafes and cabarets, in designing and teaching writing for healing workshops, in silent retreats and joining a spiritual community where I felt welcomed. But it was also writing that brought me solace, direction, inspiration, and meaning.

I offered Spiritual Memoir at the Springhouse Ministry Center. The workshop was deep, fulfilling, and enlivening. We leaped into this inquiry of our spiritual memoirs together and the writing was satisfying on a primordial level for me. It was not only about my emotional world or creative impulse; it touched down to that spiritual foundation I was unable to articulate except on the page. I thought leading the Spiritual Memoir class would be difficult, but I delighted in the way we wrote about the books that inspired us, the mentors who encouraged us, the guidance from within that kept us headed toward truth, the beauty of the world and the joy of praise and prayer. It ended up being one of my favorite classes as it restored me as much as it asked from me.

When teaching a spiritual memoir class, it is essential that the participants not only feel free to share but feel non-judged and welcomed no matter what stage of their spiritual journey they are experiencing and their system of belief. The task as facilitator is to give everyone's voice equal respect, time and attention and to acknowledge that the topic is vast and can't be covered in just four weeks…but we can begin. Creating a timeline of moments of spiritual awakening is insightful as an exercise. Sharing poems from Rumi and Hafiz can be interspersed with contemporary poems that may not address the idea of spirituality directly but point in its direction. The topic of prayer is one that each participant will relate to in unique ways and the topic of dark night of the soul must be handled with tenderness and deep listening. Sometimes the best gift we can give is to listen silently and not make a quick response. To simply say, "Thank you for sharing."

I began each session by lighting a candle and saying a brief prayer of gratitude for our willingness to show up and for the gift of creativity. I repeated often that spontaneous free writing will allow the answers to come to the surface organically as there is a tendency to over-think, to process intellectually, instead of allowing the soul to say what it needs to say. I also thought it was important if anyone could not attend a session to be able to communicate the homework assignments by email and to offer the option of emailing a final writing to me. We ended each class with blowing out the candle and thanking ourselves with our hands over our hearts for showing up. Any simple ritual: a prayer or moment of silence helps to focus the intention. A shaking of arms and legs when you all stand up, or a stretch, helps to ground back to the real world.

STRUCTURE OF SPIRITUAL MEMOIR AS A FOUR WEEK CLASS.

Topics we will cover in Spiritual Memoir:

Your childhood experience of God

When and how it changed

The first time you felt God as a presence in your adult life

Transcendent moments: Joy and terror

Finding the holy in the ordinary

Your most cherished spiritual practice: private and in community: ritual

Contact with sacred writings

Mentors, angels and miracles

Belief and doubt: a time when God failed you

Broken moments, thresholds, dark night of the soul

Praise what is unpleasant or difficult

What you want from God

God in the world

Devotion, dedication, consecration

Spiritual surrender

Prayer when prayers are not answered, when they are

God as active Presence in daily life

Session 1

POEM: Every child has known God by Hafiz

PROMPTS: Describe your beliefs as a child

What did the Divine look like, act as, to you?

From whom did you learn this?

When and how did this change?

Draw a Timeline of spiritual moments: awakenings, realizations, fir spiritual community, loss of faith, renewal of faith, etc

POEM: No More Leaving by Hafiz

PROMPT: Describe the first time you felt God as a Presence in your adult life

Transcendent moments: Joy and terror

POEM: Stone by Charles Simic

PROMPTS: What is written on my inner walls?

Describe a moment of awe that was either joyful or terrifying

Finding the holy in the ordinary

POEM: Shoveling Snow with Buddha by Billy Collins

PROMPTS: What is your daily spiritual practice? Weekly or special occasions?

How do we find the Holy when things are unjust or wrong?

POEM: A Few Reasons to Oppose the War by Lisa Suhair Majaj

PROMPT: helplessly in love....

HOMEWORK:

Write a letter of gratitude to a spiritual mentor

What has he/she given to you? How do you offer it back?

ADDITIONAL POEMS:

Praise What Comes by Jeanne Lohman

PROMPT: at the edge of the holy

Session 2: Sacred writings

PROMPT: What is the first book you think of?

What have you read, what do you read on a regular basis for spiritual succor? What are your favorite writings to uplift yourself when you feel down or doubtful? What do you read for spiritual information? How has your reading changed over time?

POEM: My Sweet Crushed Angel by Hafiz

PROMPT: Have you ever experienced an Angel or Angelic presence? What was the event? Why do you think the Angel came to you at that time? Have you ever been an angel for someone?

PROMPT: What do you think miracles are? Write about the first one and the last one you experienced

HOMEWORK:

POEM: Saladin's Begging Bowl, Be Melting Snow, The Sunrise Ruby by Rumi

PROMPTS: Write about your most cherished spiritual practice: private and in community:

Describe the setting, the structure, the way you feel, what changes in the way you feel during the practice

How do you carve time and attention from your day to do this practice?

Describe a ritual that makes you feel centered and/or that you are entering the mystery

Session 3: Dark Night of the Soul

POEM: Call Me Home by Dale Harris

PROMPT: What do you want from God? What expectations do you have that have been fulfilled or unfulfilled?

POEM: Passover by Lyn Unger

PROMPT: Write about a time when God felt absent: describe what led to it, how it felt at the time, how you view it now, what is different in your perception, attitude, or emotional being

POEM: Sweet Darkness by David Whyte

PROMPTS: Describe a time when you faced the "dark night of the soul" and whether or not you felt that it was something your soul called on you to go through, what you believe was its purpose and how it changed your faith, your practice or your relationship with others or yourself

Did you feel this was an initiation and in what way?

Did you feel that you crossed a threshold and into where?

What practice kept you most steady through this time?

What human relationship sustained you the most?

Where do you seek solace and did you find it?

Who was witness to your journey?

POEM: Lying in Wait for Happiness by Yehuda Amichai

PROMPT: my soul torn and rent

POEM: Prayer in the Strip Mall by Stuart Kestenbaum

PROMPT: Random Love

ADDITIONAL POEMS:

What do white birds say by Rumi

PROMPT: the freedom of love

Autumn, Evening by Rainer Marie Rilke

PROMPT: when you fall, Who or What holds you

Session 4: Prayer

POEM: Sometimes by Margaret Michel

POEM: Not Love Perhaps by Arthur Seymour John Tessimond

PROMPTS: Describe your prayer practice. Why is it important to you?

From whom did you learn to pray: as a child, as an adult

What has changed or shifted?

PROMPT: The day I knew

PROMPTS: Write about a time when you prayed or spoke as confession or intersession: with the

Divine or with another person

Did you feel God's Presence or answer during your time of prayer? Or afterwards?

Describe how it felt, how it impacted your belief system and your prayer practice.

Respond to one of the quotes about prayer:

"To pray is to take notice of the wonder, to regain a sense of the mystery that animates all beings, the divine margin in all attainments. Prayer is our humble answer to the inconceivable surprise of living. It is all we can offer in return for the mystery by which we live. Who is worthy to be present at the constant unfolding of time."

"I pray because God, the Shekhinah, is an outcast. I pray because God is in exile, because we all conspire to blur all signs of His presence in the present or in the past. I pray because I refuse to despair."

"We do not pray in order to be saved, we pray so that we might be worthy of being saved. Prayer should not focus on our wishes, but is a moment in

which God's intentions are reflected in us. If we are created in the image of God, each human being should be a reminder of God's presence."
— Abraham Joshua Heschel

"The prayer of a person is (in reality) a light in his heart, so whoever desires, can illuminate his heart (by means of prayers.)"—Holy Prophet Muhammad

"There are three ways in which a man expresses his deep sorrow: the man on the lowest level cries; the man on the next level is silent; the man on the highest level knows how to turn his sorrow into a song."

Look at your timeline of spiritual moments. How did prayer enter into that moment?

What was unique about each one, what was similar?

ADDITIONAL POEM: The Holy Longing by Johann Goethe

WRITING SAMPLES: written in workshop

The first time I felt God by Wendy Brown-Baez

> I felt God as a Presence inside me when I walked alone in the woods, when I danced in a meadow, allowing the joy of my body's movements to overtake me, I felt God as a desire to help others, to take care of those who suffer, I felt God as a desire to open my arms to life and to the people I felt close to, a feeling of compassionate exhilarating oneness with all life. God was dancing in my blood and my bones.

A glimpse of the holy by Wendy Brown-Baez

> Standing at the edge of meaning, wondering if God had deserted me, my glimpse of the Holy was that I still wanted God, I still yearned for intimate connection at the edge of dark wood, I didn't yet know that I would feel lost and yet be guided each step of the way. I didn't know the darkness within me had to be plucked out inch by inch to

look at, I didn't know that as I did so, the Holy would be breathing through me like a flute. A glimpse of the holy came with the prayer chaplain's words, my best friend taking me to dinner, a ride across the bay in sparkling sunlight, my grandson holding my face in his hands and saying, You have a nice face, Grandma.

RESOURCES:

Hafiz: *The Gift*, translated by Daniel Landinsky and *Drunk on the Wine of the Beloved* translated by Thomas Rain Crowe

Rumi: *The Essential Rumi,* translated by Coleman Barks and *In the Arms of the Beloved* translated by Jonathan Star

The Feminine Face of God by Sherry Ruth Anderson and Patricia Hopkins: on prayer

Poetry as a Spiritual Practice, Reading, Writing, and Using Poetry in Your Daily Rituals, Aspirations, and Intentions by Robert McDowell

Writing to Wake the Soul by Karen Hering

A PS about short writing workshops: Many experienced writers want feedback on their work. I find that 4 weeks is not enough time to give deep feedback. I begin with positive feedback (see chapter 1) but only in a workshop that is at least 6 weeks long is there the ability to offer constructive craft feedback during the final class. Perhaps this is a point that should be clarified after the first two sessions.

Writing authentically about difficult or painful topics

Where do we find the courage to tackle difficult topics? How can we remain vulnerable and transparent on the page while writing about painful memories? As a writer and as a writer instructor, I have noticed several things.

1. If we write about what is most urgent for us, it is inevitable we will tap into hurtful memories. Here is where we dig for gold, the stories that will resonate with others and where we can produce our more profoundly authentic work. Know that.

2. Practice writing in short spurts of spontaneous writing, using prompts, images, or things you obsess about and let the story you are compelled to tell surface. Read poetry to tap into the subconscious. Record your dreams. Journal about your writing process.

3. It is important to feel safe when we share. Choose a writing group or critiquing group carefully. When I lead writing workshops, we do not critique and only give positive feedback at first. We only proceed to critiquing if the participants want to publish. I share my own writing to create an atmosphere of intimacy.

4. It is okay to write crappy writing. Let go of expectations.

5. Consider the purpose: is it for self-awareness and healing or do you intend it for an audience? Ask yourself if you are ready professionally to receive a critique to improve your work.

6. If you are writing for healing, how will you explore the negative aspects of your experience? What I have learned is that you can go deeper and deeper into the story of what happened to you or you can take the branch of what did you learn, what does it mean, and how have you changed? Write about not only the trauma, but the healing story: your resilience, courage, and transformation. Be aware that you have changed in attitude, awareness or understanding. If you are writing fiction, you do not have to include it into the story but know it is there. Another idea is to write past the ending...for your eyes alone.

7. Sometimes we are writing what I call Big stories: stories that others don't have the courage or the talent or the inclination to put into words. These include topics such as domestic abuse, incest, injustice, racism, war, incarceration, suicide, illness, bullying, gender orientation, rape, mental illness, and so on. If you are voicing a truth that is powerful and empowering, can that help get you over the fear of reawakened hurt?

8. Practice in short stories, poems and essays. Try sharing them at an open mic at a friendly atmosphere such as a coffeehouse. Sometimes we are not aware of how much our stories are appreciated or how they will impact others. Develop confidence in your voice.

9. Take care of yourself: Speak with a counselor or friend, take deep breaths, stretch or do yoga, meditate or pray, sing, create positive affirmations, laugh, read something inspiring, make art

Other possibilities to get out of your head and into your heart:

- write a letter to someone you admire, expressing your admiration and gratitude
- write a letter to someone in your writing world (a writing partner, an imaginary agent or editor, a writer you admire) explaining what you are working on and your intended goals
- write a letter to a reader, explaining why you need to write your story
- If the material is too hard to write, write in third person and/or turn it into fiction

Sometimes we need the distance of third person to get our emotions on the page. Turning it into fiction will give us permission to explore other points of view and perspectives.

Positive affirmations: I am a big believer in them. I have them posted on my computer, over my desk, on my fridge, on my table altar, in my notebooks, and I pause to repeat them every day. They uplift my spirits and help strengthen my belief that my work matters.

Poetry as Transformation

There are powerful and significant moments in life filled with what is inexpressible.

In moments of transition; moments of change in our status, our beliefs, our emotions, our circumstances; moments when our ordinary world enters an alternative reality through love or death, through injustice or violation, through pain or joy, we need poetry to articulate what is deepest within, to be not only an out-pouring of language but a tender container for silence and space for the mystery to abide.

There are moments when we ache to reach out to another person but can't find the way through ordinary discourse and there are moments when we need to hear words of empathy, validation and understanding that we cannot find through normal conversation.

Poetry becomes this bridge.

Because of the way poetry is multi-layered, associative, and intuitive, it makes leaps between words, images, and concepts. It resonates even when we can't logically understand it. It is the language of dreams, the subconscious, our inner guidance, and the collective unconscious. It satisfies our human need for rhythm and imagery without having to make sense. It touches us emotionally and psychically because it expresses eternal truths and yet we appreciate the structure and words of a particular poem subjectively, as unique individuals.

I have experienced first-hand the power of poetry to guide me through moments of intense and shocking grief. When my partner died of suicide, it was my poetry writing groups that sustained me through the first weeks. When I was able to speak my truth aloud and to be heard, I felt embraced. I was not segregated by my experience but part of a community. What I could not say in normal conversation spilled out onto the page and brought me relief and healing. To write down my words and create a structure for them was an act of transformation for myself and of my life. Poetry that I read and wrote brought me back to life, to an awareness of what I had left from the ashes, and how to move forward. I have seen this happen time and again in writing groups, where tears were mingled with the ink on the page, where we read poems that moved us and cracked open our defenses so our hearts could breathe and speak freely.

To begin the journey of writing through transitions such as loss, grief or dislocation may take being in a supportive group, a safe place to feel vulnerable. It is important to be gentle with yourself while also it is important to feel safe enough to express the outrage and hurt we may be feeling. I like to use simple prompts when leading a writing workshop to take us deeper, such as "What I regret and what I don't", "What I yearn for", "The story I feel compelled to tell", and "What I lost and what I didn't lose." But the healing comes from sharing our work and being heard. For me, the process that happens in a writing circle is the discovery of our commonality. So many times I have heard someone say, "I could have written that!" It is grounding and validating to not feel we are alone, especially since so much writing is done in solitude.

I have also experienced sudden intimacy in a roomful of strangers as we shared poems in the Poetry Slam's session for remembrance and grief. The air shimmered with our tears. How healing it was to speak aloud to an audience our rage, grief, love, anger, and forgiveness through words we had chosen, words that transformed our experience into beauty and meaning.

But poetry has also played an important role in the transformation of societies and cultures. Using the image of the onion, for example, Pablo

Neruda and Miguel Hernandez made statements about poverty and justice. Hernandez wrote about the Spanish civil war and its effects on the common people and died in jail for it. Neruda was a hero to his country as he exposed the tyranny of fascism and endured years of exile. I think of the censorship Anna Akmatova suffered, or the death of Afghani poet Nadia Anjuman. Iranian poet Simin Behahani was held under house arrest for her criticism of those in power. Poetry binds people together as a nation and as a force of change because it digs down to the deeper level where we have in common the desire for truth, mercy, and compassion, for being visible and accountable, for feeling loved and honored, for growth and becoming.

Poetry also fulfills our need for play and humor. A child is delighted with the silliness of Dr. Seuss or nursery rhymes. Poems can make us laugh at the absurdity of life, poems wittily point out our human failings, poems soar with gratitude at beauty. The gratification of our innate human need to express ourselves, to communicate, to commune, is the way we build community, the way we step out over the abyss of our essential solitariness to see that we are held in a web of light.

Because poetry is intuitive and does not have to be linear, it can subtly transform our very molecules as the words touch our deepest core and emotions, as words take us on a transcendent voyage out of our emotions to the place of awe and magic, where we realize we are interconnected. Words spoken with the rhythm of love can comfort, heal, inspire, uplift and mend. Words spoken with the joy of discovery can upend us so that we see the world with fresh vision and new shifts in meaning.

I have experienced both the sense of weaving that moment when we breathe together and that moment of having the "top of my head" taken off, as Emily Dickenson said, when I could barely move, where the only place to go was deep within my own soul to catch up to the words that had moved me and transformed me. May you have the chance to have this extraordinary experience. May you be anointed with the blessing of poetry that is authentically true and fiercely tender.

THE BENEFITS OF USING POETRY AS A JUMP START FOR WRITING:

Poetry provides a cultural context and expressive model that supports openness and emotional honesty.

It connects us to our intuitive imagination.

Reading and writing poetry is a natural process for people in pain.

Poetry provides a private experience where an individual can control the outcome.

Writing poetry is joyful and self-affirming even if the topic is painful.

It is a skill that we can continue to access.

It is a way of connecting with others through reading and publishing.

(excerpted from Writing with At-Risk Youth: the PONGO Teen Writing Method)

PART TWO:

MEMOIR: Beyond Generating Material to Crafting Stories

Memoir VS Fiction

When I wrote my memoir *Flowers in the Wind*, I wanted to document the things that had happened, all of my memories, before they faded but I wrote it with my experience as a fiction writer. I wanted the reader to be invested enough to want to find out what happened to me. I hoped the reader would feel resonance in the choices I made. As I approached publishers with the first chapters, it became evident that the story read as a novel instead of a memoir because I hadn't written my reflections on my experience from the viewpoint of my present self.

The reason people read memoir is to connect deeply with someone they either admire or identify with, to gain insight into their own lives. The memoirs that really touch people's hearts are the ones in which readers not only imagine themselves in that person's shoes, but can be uplifted, inspired, provoked, and connected to a universal truth. In which their hearts are pierced by the honesty and courage of the story-teller, and the story of resilience despite all odds.

I wanted the reader to come to their own conclusions but my writer friends told me that if I wanted the book to be read that way, I should write it as a novel. For this particular project, it would mean removing huge sections of the book. It would need tighter pacing. I wrote it with a natural spiraling rhythm of feeling lost and lonely, allowing decisions that I didn't agree with to be made for me, rebelling and striking out to be independent, then returning to where I felt accepted and loved. This might make it in a novel from the 19th century but not the 21st, sad to say.

I had taken out all the words of self-reflection and now I had to put them back in. When I started to work with an editor, I learned that I had to explain our lifestyle more specifically. She didn't understand why certain choices were made.

The difference between reflection and take-away is that reflection is a moment of inner musing to make sense of the experience but the take-away is a moment of connection with the reader, where you offer something that speaks heart to heart. Brooke Warner writes, "If you're a reader of memoir and you've experienced a really good takeaway, you'll recognize these moments as the ones where you experienced a chill, a deep level of connection, or when you needed to put the book down for a second to sink into the powerful truth the author has just revealed."

Both reflection and take-away must be interwoven through-out, little jewels of insight embedded in the text. My editor suggested that I consider the theme of each chapter as well as the overarching theme of the entire book, a thread that runs consistently throughout while each chapter may have varied undertones. My memoir is the story of how I lived communally for ten years. We took in the homeless and traveled worldwide by hitchhiking. As we succumbed to the manipulations of one powerful, charismatic man, things began to unravel. My major theme is how I lost my identity in order to fit in and how I gained it back, how I overcame the constant criticism of not being good enough to stand up for myself. The minor themes include the challenges of single mothering, desire for love, manipulation by a powerful man, traveling by faith, the desire to serve the less fortunate. The universal truth is that we all want to belong, to feel welcomed, to come home, to know we are enough. This journey is harder if we are artistic, social rebels, pioneers, peace-niks, visionaries, and have a strong desire for social justice and true equality. We often give up parts of ourselves, sometimes our whole selves, our freedom, our money, our voice, our conscience, our beliefs, to fit in, to be part of, rather than demanding that the group change or to leave the shelter of the group to go it alone. Reclaiming ourselves is essential to move forward after a severe and devastating loss when we no longer fit or are expelled or can't put up with the inconsistencies any longer. For me, the life I choose was meant to be my life *for the rest of my life.*

This section of my memoir takes place when one of the "sisters" and I and our children have been sent off after being told that we were not disciplined enough to live with the group. I was seven months pregnant at the time and had a twenty-month-old son. I was determined to improve in order to return to the fold but was mostly consumed with finding places to stay. We ended up at her family home until I was invited to return to the group in Santa Fe.

Snow started to fall as we pulled in to the Santa Fe Greyhound Bus station. Diane answered the phone and said someone would come to fetch me. I burst into tears when I saw Brett coming through the door. My entire body trembled with relief as we greeted each other with a warm embrace. I shoved the box into a locker. He swung Yoan up onto his shoulders, I tucked Manoah into my arms and we set off for the hostel.

The familiar atmosphere of homeless men sitting around the TV while supper bubbled on the stove. A hot cup of coffee served by Tiffany with a gracious smile. Hugs and exclamations over the newborn—and being welcomed the way a guest is welcomed. The insecurity bubbled up immediately. As sharp as that IV needle driven into my arm. *How could I have ever thought I could fit in here?*

The next day Russell escorted me to the other house, the private house where Ben and Marian stayed, in an atmosphere of study and contemplation. I was an outsider. My room was in the basement, dark and hidden away. Yoan was expected to sit still through the morning readings rather than go off to play. All the children sat with us, including the youngest. I had never forced Yoan to do anything in his life. He wailed and squirmed. I took him outside and scolded him, disrupting the somber atmosphere.

My first conversation with Ben included being chastised for how many things I had acquired, how we were dressed (Yoan in corduroy overalls rather than jeans) and my utter lack of discipline.

…I was scoured by Ben Oren from top to bottom. The clothes I wore (pastels), my relationship with Cristopher (all sweet, no substance), and my attitudes (spoiled princess), my lack of understanding and respect for my elders, my lack of obedience and devotion. Ben repeated his litany of my personality. "You are a beautiful girl but you have cotton candy in your head. It's probably not your fault but you have to change…you have to change. You are vain and presumptuous and that has to change."

"But what can I do?" I wailed.

His face folded into a severe frown but Marian stepped in.

"Stephanie and Anna have just sent us a postcard from Missoula where they have been helping out at a place that feeds people. They just rented an apartment and want someone to come up there. You can leave tomorrow if you want."

I slowly stood up, relieved that I had somewhere to go. Ben turned away. "Thank you," he said sarcastically. I had no gratitude for what they were doing for me, pointing out the changes I needed to make. I was too hurt and humiliated.

I stayed at the hostel for the next two days while an attempt was made to raise bus fare. I trudged through slushy piles of snow, but I had used all my options in the fall. Finally Diane informed me that Salvador would hitchhike with me. It was the dead of winter and Manoah, now called Ezekiel, was three weeks old. My faith was being tested and I did not falter. By placing myself and my children in God's Hands, I would be escorted every step of the way to safety. The only way to go was forward. Toward Montana.

Looking back, I can't believe I didn't protest or take my kids and get out of there. The heart truly makes no sense. Was I holding on to those moments when I felt connected, bonded, or was it the promise held out to us that we would become pure of heart and able to make miracles? Was it strength or exhaustion? No one ever shared their doubts or worries with me, but people would leave, usually quietly. The immediacy of finding rent and cooking and cleaning and caring for children, or those moments of euphoric companionship, took away our ability to discern whether or not the Scriptures being poured over us every morning were truly transforming us into Christ-like disciples capable of healing or saving souls. We wanted to be "good servants worthy of our reward" and "inherit the Kingdom prepared for us." Of course we did. *I* did.

I don't know if this take-away, that strong desire to be good while never being quite good enough, is one that will pierce the hearts of my readers. But every woman who has suffered demeaning abuse, every man who has put up with humiliation at the hand of a boss, will recognize that sometimes we ignore our inner intuition for the hope of acceptance, love, and redemption. It would take more than a scolding about the pastels I was wearing to wake me up to the dangerous power of control and condescension.

As writers, we must remember that we are telling a story as a way to build a bridge between ourselves and the reader, one that is tender and sturdy, fragile and invincible: the thread between our hearts.

Writing Memoir: WHY?

We know that the stories we are compelled to write are the stories that haunt us, the ones that won't let go. For many of us, these stories are based on memories. We write memoirs in order to reflect on our past and make sense of it, to share our experiences and the insights gained, and to capture those moments of joy or terror or revelation that make us who we are. I believe every one of us has a powerful and engaging story to tell. Writing itself is a therapeutic tool, can help us gain insight on the past and see our patterns and choices so we can coach ourselves toward the future. Telling our stories gives them meaning and validates who we are, connects us to each other and the human community. However, the dedicated composing and editing that is the core of how we get it down on paper (or on the screen) is where many of us give up, blocked, frightened, or exhausted.

To write from a deeper place of vulnerability, becoming open to the pain of one's memories, and yet to remain with a soft heart despite the feelings of rage, guilt, grief, and denial that might arise, to allow the process to take you over the edge to where you might see the threads of your life in an intricate weaving instead of a tangled mess, takes patience, practice, and using writer's tools such as writing in a group, taking a workshop, and using writing exercises from books such as *Pain and Possibility* by Gabriella Rico or any of the Artist Way series by Julia Cameron. It may be a writer's retreat with the ability to focus on the emotions that are surfacing rather than responding to those who don't understand the intensity of this work. There are scholarships and residencies if you feel daunted by financial considerations. Or it may be as simple as reading back through your journals or calling someone to confirm details, playing a song from that era, flipping through a photo album, or returning to the place where the memories were born. Recording your dreams, meditating, and even eating the same foods that you once enjoyed might trigger something. Memories are built from our senses. For me these include the crunchy taste of falafel in Israel, the scent of garbage in the Mercado in Oaxaca, the day everyone in the circle wore blue, how the sea washed cold against our feet, the perfume of grandmother's garden, the rumbling of buses below the window.

There is a time for gathering memories and putting them down on the page and there is a time to craft the words into an art form. What makes good writing? What makes a memoir refreshing and accessible? How will readers connect to your story?

Good writing comes from a place of both courage and vulnerability. To show our human side—our failures, mistakes, doubts and fears, our desires, fantasies, and hopes and dreams—is a way to connect with readers. We must be a sympathetic character and we may have to step back from our story in a more objective way to ensure that we are revealing ourselves as flawed and yet determined or resilient human beings. We must have the courage to tell the truth, despite those nagging voices that worry what others might think, in particular the other people in our story. Will they be offended, will they be shocked by our revelations, will they be hurt? You must write the story as if no one else will read it but you must edit the story for the whole world to hear.

In other words, if you are writing about real people, you must be aware of your motivations. Tracy Seely, author of *My Ruby Slippers: The Road Back to Kansas* writes that it is essential to have clean motives and transparency. If the person in your story is necessary and yet his/her actions are shown in an unfavorable light, what are the possible ways to handle this?

Some writers change the names and identifying characteristics of their characters. Some writers let the people in their stories read about themselves ahead of time. Some ask permission. If you are writing about a well-known public figure or place or business, your publisher may want to have you consult a lawyer. If you are writing about close family members that can be identified, you may want to consult a lawyer or ask their permission. But ultimately it is why you are telling this story that will influence the outcome.

At the 2014 AWP conference panel on writing personal essays, each member of the panel had a different answer to the question of how to deal with this issue, ranging from "I did not ask permission ahead of time and I was surprised by the support I received" to "Yes, my family member was upset, but not for the reasons I thought he would be." When you publish, reactions may not be supportive or someone may be hurt and it is up to you as the writer to decide if it is something you can live with. Are you compelled to tell this story? Should you change it to fiction? Personally, I believe if you write with the intention of sharing your healing or transformation or overcoming and surviving, the power of the story will transcend other people's reactions. By the way, the panel also mentioned that you must never assume someone will not read your work because they don't read literary journals or small magazines or on-line journals as the internet spreads our words everywhere and you never know where it will pop up.

Mark Fowler in his blog "Rights of Writers" writes: "Remember, to be actionable, the disclosure must be of private facts that would be highly offensive to a reasonable person. Most memoirs don't venture into that territory. Moreover, book editors often tell their authors to write the truth and let the in-house lawyers figure out how the truth—or at least most of it—can be safely published."

Here is full disclosure: I changed everyone's names in *Flowers in the Wind*. Many of the people I wrote about are no longer alive but their family members are. I did not assume that anyone who once was a part of our alternative lifestyle would want publicity. I told my story through my own interpretation and take full responsibility for that. However, I choose not to ask permission. I feel that this is a story that speaks to those who tried alternative lifestyles and they will understand our flaws and failures came from youthful immaturity. The "leader" who betrayed us was someone I loved as well as grew to resent and despise....but he is no longer alive.

Ingredients for a well-crafted memoir:

- A sympathetic main character
- Vividly depicted scenes: description that use sensual details, dialogue and energy that move from conflict to resolution, from quest to discovery
- Emotional tension created from the character's desires and needs and ability or inability to fulfill them.
- Increasing sense of drama/conflict: choices, realizations and revelations, patterns to be broken or adhered to, loss and hope, or inner and outer conflict. Make readers aware of what might be lost and why the character's decisions are important.
- A satisfying ending and a mixture of reflection and take-away: What do you want readers to leave with? Stories that move us move from conflict, challenge, quest, question or problem to resolution, healing, transformation, change of attitude or change of understanding, discovery or deeper questions. How did you change from your experience? How will the reader be changed by reading your story?

RESOURCES

Writing the Memoir, From Truth to Art by Judith Barrington, The Eighth Mount Press, 2002

The Situation and the Story: The Art of Personal Narrative, by Vivian Gornick, Farrar, Straus and Giroux, 2001

The Heart and Craft of Lifestory Writing: How to Transform Memories into Meaningful Stories, by Sharon Lippincott, Lighthouse Point Press 2007

One Year to a Writing Life: Twelve Lessons to Deepen Every Writer's Art and Craft by Susan Tiberghien, Da Capo Press, 2007

The Autobiographers' Handbook: The 826 National Guide to Writing Your Memoir by Jennifer Traig, Henry Holt and Company, 2008

Breathe Life into Your Life Story: How to Write a Story People Will Want to Read, by Dawn Thurstone Signature Books, 2007

Writing Memoir: How do I find my voice?

The difference between fiction and memoir is not only the structure that the writing takes, but the fact that your readers have to resonate with *you* as the main character. Your voice must reflect who you are, not a persona, and yet at the same time, you are the protagonist and have a persona on the page. You have experiences, adventures, struggles and revelations, insights and self-awareness leading to transformation, healing or connection. Or more questions, insight and acceptance.

Your voice is distinctive and your friends recognize your voice immediately on the phone. How do we access our unique voice when we are writing? Or how do we know when we have found our voice? How do we walk that tightrope between telling our story so that others will feel what we felt and yet with enough subjectivity that we are sharing a story and not a therapy session? How do we maintain urgency while showing the wider picture?

I would ask what has the most emotional energy for you? What are your passions, fears, and joys? What is hard to write about? What do you avoid writing about? And what is your personal point of view on the world?

I teach what I call self-reflective writing in Writing for Healing classes and I use prompts to start spontaneous timed writing. I have discovered than when I read a poem and then dive into my feelings, my writing is lyrical, flows easily, touches my core beliefs, includes specific images and details, and ends on a positive note usually with a spiritual insight. When I use a writing exercise of craft such as writing a setting with a characters or characters, add dialogue, decision or a sudden change, or work with a prompt grounded in facts, I struggle and meander back and forth all over the page. There is no sense of what drives the writing. I will need to edit and revise.

My voice is attuned to my deepest feelings and core beliefs: life is full of terror, grief, and beauty and has meaning, love, and hope; each moment is a gift and holy in its own perfection, not matter how broken or bruised it may appear. My essential nature is to look for the extraordinary in the ordinary.

I remind writers that writing is a practice. A practice means that we are practicing all the time, not only when we are working on a short story or memoir or poem. By writing exercises to warm up the intuitive imagination, we strike gold: something can be woven into a larger piece.

I use a simple exercise to help writers access their material. We begin with writing numbers down the page in 5 sections such as this:

1. _____

2. _____

3. _____

4. _____

5. _____

and then I suggest a category for each section. We write what comes to mind quickly and spontaneously without over-thinking. I move from one category to the next quickly.

The first category is always things I love because that one is easy. The following may be:

- things that annoy me
- things I regret
- times I lost something important

- things I will never forgive
- moments that changed my life
- places I hang out
- people I admire
- times I had to make a decision
- times I took a risk
- things I left behind
- blessings

For example: things I love:

hearing the sound of Spanish around me

the beach

my grandsons

poetry

The exercise can be extended with specific details:

the beach in Puerto Vallarta at sunset with a cold drink in my hands

reading a story together with my grandsons

poems that opened my heart

Often then I give a prompt:

- What I will never forget
- I remember
- At that moment
- The first time

The idea is to access right brain intuition by accessing memories but in a quick overview so that what is most compelling comes to the surface. Now we have 25 topics to write about; all of these are emotionally charged topics. Circle one and write for ten minutes. The exercise can be repeated; allow new memories to arise. I have taught it often and each time, what I focus on will shift depending on what items have filled my list.

I once made the mistake of changing the introduction of my memoir after attending a workshop on dynamic first pages. I had originally started with the impact of the '60s, but moved that to another section in order to begin with the first time I took a trip to Mexico. However, I had cut off my own voice as surely as if I had strangled myself. I had to think again of how my story really started. It began when I visited Arlington Cemetery as a 6th grader and become a pacifist, a realization that would lead me to the anti-war movement during the Viet Nam War and later, to seek my tribe of those who believed as I did.

Change to "dynamic first sentence":

The first time I crossed the border into Mexico, I was eight months pregnant and single. Carin invited me to accompany her as she drove Roxanna, Irene and their children, Chandra and Carissa, from Santa Fe to Juarez. From there, they would hitch-hike farther south. I knew members of the group traveled to spread the Good News, imitating the first-century Disciples of Jesus. Despite the discomfort of the baby somersaulting in my belly and constant pressure on my bladder, I agreed.

Change to Claiming My Story:

When I was in sixth grade, our class took a field trip from my hometown of Lancaster, Pennsylvania, to Washington, DC. I don't remember much about filing through the White House, although I do remember being impressed by the size of the Senate chambers and the Lincoln Memorial. However, it was the visit to Arlington National Cemetery that changed my life.

As I looked over the thousands of soldiers' graves that fanned out to the horizon, a feeling swept over me of profoundly disturbing sorrow. *This is wrong*, I thought. The sight of those tombstones fanning out to the horizon gave me an epiphany. At that moment, a clear vision transformed me into a pacifist. My heart was broken open by those white tombstones and it changed my perception of everything.

But little by little,

as you left their voices behind,

the stars began to burn

through the sheets of clouds,

and there was a new voice

which you slowly

recognized as your own

—Mary Oliver

Finding your voice takes vulnerability and the courage to be yourself. With practice, you will tap into the story you are compelled to tell. That story that haunts you and will not let you rest until it is told. That's your voice.

Another tip: Write about a topic that resonates with you either because it makes you laugh, cry or rage. Write about a moment that changed your life: your perceptions, your place, your relationships, your identity, or your awareness.

Writing Memoir: Pacing

When we speak of pacing in fiction, we are talking about an interweave of narrative, description, dialogue, conflicts and decisions. The plot pulls the story along and keeps the reader turning the pages. In some ways, how much or how little of these elements you use is subjective. Consider what you like when you read. For example, I prefer limited dialogue. I enjoy intricate descriptions of the characters' inner thoughts and feelings, information that lets me know why people react the way they do. I love descriptions filled with sensual imagery and unusual metaphors or similes. Others prefer lots of dialogue, limited description and fast-paced action.

When we begin to write our memoirs, we may not be thinking about plot. We may be writing down the basic story of what happened and what we think about it. If we use the same craft elements for memoir as fiction, we will write something dynamic, fascinating and true to the holistic arch of the story.

The pace of the story is determined by the descriptions. Too many and the reader will start to disconnect; too few and it will not be vivid enough. Descriptions carry us along and work best interspersed with dialogue and plot. It's all in the details. As a writer, you need to transport readers into your setting and time period as well as to make connections to universal truths.

Description, dialogue and decisions move the plot along. The main character is you: how do you show a personality worthy of your reader's emotional investment? Start with vulnerability and courage on the page. Be willing to take emotional risks. Then through description, dialogue, and the decisions made, you show that you are unique and yet flawed; that you acted on desires and sought solutions that may or may not have worked; that you are a real person with inner conflicts, quirky personality traits, motivated by the same things that motivate us all: to discover the key to understanding, the gift of insight, the ability to change. You want the reader to see the world through your eyes. At the same time, this is not a persuasive essay. This is your life, in all its messy twists and turns and wrong assumptions and judgments and aha! moments and love and tenderness and awakening. Nevertheless, you want to write in a way that makes sense to readers, that follows either the structure of before, during and after (before I was hurt, unhappy, unhealthy, struggling, abused, confused, etc and then I did this and this happened and afterwards, I was healed; found joy, acceptance and friendship; became a better person; became stronger, etc) whether or not you write in a linear time frame or use backstory. You can use the Hero's journey as a template: the call to adventure, the encounter with guides and mentors, given seemingly impossible tasks and a protagonist you must conquer (even if it is your own doubts, fears, and weaknesses), leading to receiving the reward of insight, wisdom, or change, and bringing it back to the world.

Tension moves the story along. Tension is created through inner and / or outer conflicts. Inner conflicts are psychological or moral—desires, choices, reactions, beliefs, hopes and dreams. Outer conflicts include relationships, the sequence of events, heritage, family expectations, social-historical context, and challenges such as health challenges or outer circumstances such as poverty, war, famine, or racism. The desire to be a free spirit while my culture and family told me that I needed to earn a living is one of the conflicts that underpin my stories of growing into adulthood. Or the tension between pleasing a loved one I disagree with while suppressing a desire to be heard and respected is another.

Decisions are what tighten and invigorate the plot. Decisions are ways the character makes choices that determine their fate, such as where they end up, how they feel, their relationships, and their gained insight or wisdom or change of attitude, perception or understanding.

Dialogue is natural; it is the way we interact with the world. It can be as simple as a few sentences. Too much dialogue and the piece will seem weightless and insubstantial. It can be used to illuminate the setting, tell the back story, show a relationship between characters, give information about the characters or circumstances or the characters' beliefs and attitudes. It captures the nuances of the characters' speech patterns, especially if there is an accent, special verbal ticks, or particularities. It can show where a character is from, what they know, and what they want.

Each character should have a unique viewpoint and should sound unlike the others. Characters can be defined based on what they ask or tell as well as what they refuse to reveal.

Dialogue can replace long narratives to move the pace along with information that is important but not essential to tell in detail. It can transition between time periods. It can heighten tension, as when two characters disagree, and it sheds light on how others perceive you.

Plot keeps the reader turning the pages. Plots move from a conflict, challenge, quest or question, to resolution, transformation or change of attitude, perception or understanding. The main character is changed in some way.

Just like fiction, a personal essay or memoir has to include an inciting incident. Something has to happen to set off a physical, emotional, and/or intellectual reaction. For example, if you wrote an argument between your brother and your mother in which your mother wants your brother to stop going out late at night, you'd want to denote what started that argument and whether the argument was about safety or about seeking control in the family or generational and personality conflicts.

Memoir is both a story of your inner knowledge *and* your experiences of interaction with the world: family, friends, lovers, mentors, guides. You also have antagonists: those who tighten the tension by misunderstandings, physical or emotional mistreatment, judgement, intolerance, or even by being overbearing and meddlesome. Your antagonist could be your loved ones with expectations or friends who mislead you or demand misplaced loyalty. He/she can be a mentor who is competitive or a spiritual guide who misuses his power.

All these elements can be woven together in a way that bring you as the character to life but also keep the reader engaged and on the edge of their seat to see what happens to you.

A surprise delights the reader but it has to seem authentic and realistic. In other words, the events leading up to it must point toward it in some way. Surprises can include synchronicity, messages from other dimensions that come true, incongruent emotional reactions, unexpected reactions from characters or unexpected plot twists. However, use surprise with caution. If it is too strange, it can seem jarring and inauthentic.

Not all endings are positive and may leave a question unanswered. The reader wants to see that the protagonist gained something from the experience. We read stories to learn how others cope, especially with loss, uncertainty, failure, illness and trauma.

Every good story changes someone: the main character, a secondary character or the reader. We want the reader to have a shift of perspective. It may be as simple as remembering we lose our naiveté and innocence as we mature. It may be our resilience despite difficult circumstances. It may be a call to social justice or awakening to spiritual truth.

"The king died and the queen died is a story. The king died and the queen died of grief is a plot." —E. M. Forester

What do you think?

APPENDIX

Additional Resources:

Books on Writing and Writing Life & Writing Poetry – gleaned from WOM-PO List

Addonizio, Kim and Dorianne Laux, *The Poet's Companion*

Addonizio, Kim *Ordinary Genius*

Atwood, Margaret *Negotiating with the Dead*

Baer, William *Writing Metrical Poetry: Contemporary Lessons for Mastering Traditional Forms*

Bell, James Scott *Plot and Structure*

Behn, Robin & Chase Twichell, *The Practice of Poetry*

Boisseau, Michelle / Wallace, Robert *Writing Poems*

Branden, Dorothea *Becoming a Writer*

Burroughway, Janet *Writing Fiction or Imaginative Writing*

Carper Thomas and Derek Attridge, *Meter and Meaning: An Introduction to Rhythm in Poetry*

Dacey, Philip and David Jauss, *Strong Measures*

Corn, Alfred *The Poem's Heartbeat*

Clark, Kevin *A Mind's Eye: A Guide to Writing Poetry.*

Pinsky, Robert *The Sounds of Poetry: A Brief Guide*

DeSalvo, Louise *The Art of Slow Writing: Reflections on Time, Craft and Creativity*

Dillard, Annie *The Writing Life*

Doty, Mark *The Art of Description* (and others in "Art of" series published by Graywolf Press)

Finch, Annie *Poems in Forms by Contemporary Women; A Poet's Craft*

Finch, Annie and Katherine Varnes, *An Exaltation of Forms*

Fletcher, Angus *A New Theory for American Poetry*

Friedman, Bonnie *Writing Past Dark: Envy, Fear, Distraction, and Other Dilemmas in the Writer's Life*

Fry, Stephen *The Ode Less Traveled*

Hamill, Sam *A Poet's Work*

Higginson, William J. and Harter, Penny *The Haiku Handbook: How to Write, Teach and Appreciate Haiku.*

Hirshfield, Jane *Nine Gates*

Hollander, John *Rhyme's Reason: A Guide to English Verse*

Johnston, Brett Anthony *Naming the World*

King, Stephen *On Writing*

Koch, Kenneth *Wishes, Lies Dreams*

Kowit, Steve *In the Palm of Your Hand*

Kooser, Ted *The Poetry Home Repair Manual*

Lamott, Annie *Bird by Bird*

Levertov, Denise *The Poet in the World; Light Up the Cave*

Lockward, Diane *The Crafty Poet*

Mason, David and John Frederick Nims, *Western Wind, An Introduction to Poetry*

Mayes, Francis *Discovery of Poetry*

Meinke, Peter *The Shape of Poetry*

Metzger, Deena *Writing for Your Life*

Oliver, Mary *Poetry Handbook*

Olsen, Tillie *Silences*

Padgett, Ron *Handbook of Poetic Forms*

Palumo, Dennis *Writing from the Inside Out: Transforming Your Psychological Blocks to Release the Writer Within*

Parrott, E.O. *How to Be Well-Versed in Poetry*

Ponsot, Marie *Beat Not the Poor Desk*

Reufle, Mary *Madness, Rack and Honey*

Rich, Adrienne *What is Found There*

Rukeyser, Muriel *Life of Poetry*

Stafford, William *Writing the Australian Crawl*

Steele, Timothy *All the Fun's in How You Say a Thing*

Turco, Lewis *The New Book of Forms*

Ueland, Brenda *If You Want to Write*

Weldon, Fay *Letters to Alice on First Reading Jane Austen*

Welty, Eudora *One Writer's Beginnings*

Wiggerman, Scott *Wingbeats I* and *II*

Wooldredge, Susan *Poemcrazy*

Young, Dean *The Art of Recklessness*

Craft of Nonfiction

Barrington, Judith *Writing the Memoir: From Truth to Art*

Gutkind, Lee *The Art of Creative Nonfiction.*

Lopate, Philip *The Art of the Personal Essay*

Gornick, Vivian *The Situation and the Story: The Art of Personal Narrative*

Vivian, Robert *On the Meditative Essay*

Silverman, Sue *The Meandering River*

Zinsser, William *On Writing Well: The Classic Guide to Writing Nonfiction*

Craft of Fiction

Bly, Carol *The Passionate Accurate Story: Making Your Heart's Truth into Literature*

Burroway, Jane *Writing Fiction: A Guide to Narrative Craft*

Olen Butler, Robert *From Where You Dream: The Process of Writing Fiction*

Gardner, John *The Art of Fiction: Notes on Craft for Young Writers.*

Lerner, Betsy *The Forest for the Trees: An Editor's Advice to Writers.*

Stern, Jerome *Making Shapely Fiction*

Screenwriting

McKee, Robert *Story: Substance, Structure, Style and the Principles of Screenwriting*

Truby, John *Anatomy of Story: 22 Steps to Becoming a Master Storyteller*

More Books on Writing:

Bane, Rosanne: *Around the Writer's Block*

George, Elizabeth *Write Away*

Heard, Georgia *Writing Toward Home*

Hemley, Robin *Turning Life Into Fiction*

Hering, Karen *Writing to Wake the Soul*

Le Quinn, Ursula *Steering the Craft*

Murray, Donald *Shoptalk: Learning to Write with Writers*

Prose, Francine *Reading Like a Writer: A guide for people who love books and for those who want to read them*

Sloane, William *The Craft of Writing*

Schneider, Pat *Writing Alone and with Others*

Strunk William and EB White: *The Elements of Style*

Curtis Swallow, Pamela *A Writer's Notebook: The Ultimate Guide to Creative Writing*

Vogler, Christopher *The Writer's Journey, Mythic Structure for Writers*

MY PERSONAL WRITER'S TOOLBOX AND HOW I USE IT:

The Writer's Toolbox:

Julia Cameron: *The Artist Way*

Natalie Goldberg: *Writing Down the Bones*

Gabrielle Rico: *Writing the Natural Way, Pain and Possibility*

Louis DeSalvo: *Writing as a Way of Healing*

Victoria Nelson: *On Writer's Block*

Naomi Epel: *The Observation Deck, A Tool Kit for Writers*

Judy Reeves: *A Writer's Book of Days*

These books are on my shelf. Whenever I feel I need a boost, a reminder of why I continue to practice a discipline that can be lonely, difficult, and frustrating, I open one of these books and read a page or two. These books have ideas for writing exercises, observations about other artists and writers and anecdotes on the writing life.

Poets & Writers Magazine www.pw.org

For prompts and writing ideas:

http://www.creativewritingprompts.com

http://www.writersdigest.com/prompts

For a community of women writers:

www.wow-womenonwriting.com: advice, workshops, contests, and blog tours

www.shewrites.com: tips, groups, ability to blog

For a community of readers and writers: www.goodreads.com: a community to discuss books. Your profile enables you to post book reviews or your own books, blog, and add events. You can join groups and make comments on book reviews. You can submit to a monthly poetry contest, get critiques and network with other writers.

www.awpwriter.org: AWP conferences include hundreds of literary journals, small presses and publishing companies in the book fair, workshops, panels, readings and the opportunity to network with thousands of writers.

About blogging: it is a way to get your work posted on line and direct friends and fans to your work. It's free and easy, with templates to guide you. You can post photos and have readers leave comments. Word of warning: some presses consider work posted on a blog to be published. Blogspot.com or wordpress.com.

Poetry:

Academy of American Poets: poets.org

www.poetryfoundation.org

Motionpoems.com: Poems set to graphics and music

Diane Lockward publishes a monthly newsletter http://www.dianelockward.com/gpage1.html

I didn't know that if you want to write, you must follow your desire to write. And that your writing will help you unravel the knots in your heart. I didn't know that you could write simply to take care of yourself, even if you have no desire to publish your work. I didn't know that if you want to become a writer, eventually you'll learn through writing—and only through writing—all you need to know about your craft. And that while you're learning, you're engaging in soul-satisfying, deeply nurturing labor. —Louis De Salvo

Discovering Gold

Because the sea is gold

and this moment is all that we have—

Because we quarreled, then kissed

we find easy bliss on the sunset beach.

The sun dressed in gold lamé

for his evening bow and we lay on earth's

sandy breast while the sky put the birds to bed

for a midnight romp of stars. The moon

is a laughing fool in a universe so vast

we are no more than a wink, a flash

of green you say only the keenly observant

can see when it halos above the water

to bless the coming darkness. Because we

are safe with the rest of our lives to fill

like blanks in a crossword puzzle, following

the trail of choices and clues, this moment

is good as gold, to be claimed like pearls

from the river, each one perfect as itself

each one indifferent to time.

PROMPT: an unexpected blessing

Wendy Brown-Báez is a writer, teacher, performance poet and installation artist. Wendy is the author of the novel *Catch a Dream*, poetry collection *Ceremonies of the Spirit* and poetry chapbook *transparencies of light*. She has published poetry and prose in numerous literary journals, such as *Borderlands, The Litchfield Review, Lavandería, Mizna, Minnetonka Review, Water~Stone Review, Tiferet*, anthologies such as *The Chrysalis Reader, Wising Up Press*, and *The Heart of All That Is* and in on-line journals such as *Interfaithings, Talking Writing* and *Duende*. Her article *Why We Write: The Wounded and Enduring* was published in Poets & Writers July/August 2014 issue and her creative non-fiction essay won Women's National Book Association's 2016 national contest.

Wendy was awarded McKnight, MN State Arts Board, and Saint Louis Park Art & Culture grants to teach writing workshops for youth in crisis and in non-profits. She continues to teach at Pathways and in prisons with Minnesota Prison Writing Workshop. She facilitates workshops in community spaces such as healing centers, libraries, churches, schools, cafes, yoga studios, spiritual centers, museums, and arts organizations.

Wendy is available to speak to your writer's group and to lead writing workshops at your organization, community center, spiritual center or class. She also presents Cultivating Resiliency Through Writing workshops and is available to discuss how writing for healing can be used as a resource for integrative medicine.

If you are unable to find any of the poems mentioned in this book, please contact her through her website. All poems are available on line except Famous Kisses and Discovering Gold, included in the book.

To learn more about her work, go to: www.wendybrownbaez.com